UNEXPECTED ANSWERS

BARBARA BARTOCCI

Our Sunday Visitor Publishing Division
Our Sunday Visitor, Inc.
Huntington, Indiana 46750

Acknowledgments

The majority of the stories appearing in this work first appeared in the following publications:

♣ *Reader's Digest* (Letters Home From War / October 1982; Let Go and Live / October 1989; A Gift From the Heart ["Real Ways to Say You Care"] / November 1990; The Unexpected Answer / September 1984; The Power of Hercules / November 1986; and Golden Scrapbooks of the Mind / December 1987)

♣ *The Catholic Digest* (My Father's Last Gift / August 1991; Old Tom Was No Quitter / April 1985; The Hour That Changed My Life / August 1983; GrandJack Held On / March 1986; One-Minute Prayer / March 1992; I'm a Recovering Perfectionist! / November 1989; Good-bye to the Money-God / March 1990; The Splendid Joy of Living Simply / September 1991; A Gift From the Woman in White / November 1990; and The Magic Word for 'God Within' / May 1988)

♣ *Glamour* (I Had Money and Success; What Was Wrong? / August 1983)

♣ *Good Housekeeping* (Leap Into the Light / June 1990)

♣ *Woman's Day* (Seventy Times Seven / December 1993)

♣ *Guideposts* (Picking Up the Pieces / September 1986)

♣ *St. Anthony's Messenger* (God, My Mother, and Me / July 1989)

♣ *The Liguorian* (Soul on Sabbatical / March 1985)

♣ Original stories (My Grandparents' House; The Waiting Parent; Zigzag Faith; and Love in Unexpected Places).

The author and publisher are grateful for material contained in this work that originally appeared in various publications and has been adapted to one extent or another. If any copyrighted materials have been inadvertently used in this work without proper credit being given in one form or another, please notify Our Sunday Visitor in writing so that future printings of this work may be corrected accordingly.

International Standard Book Number: 0-87973-742-5
Library of Congress Catalog Card Number: 93-87104

Cover design by Rebecca J. Heaston

PRINTED IN THE UNITED STATES OF AMERICA

Dedicated to Sony, John, and Andy:
my dear children . . . my dear friends.

Table of Contents

Introduction / 7

GROWING THROUGH LOSS / 10

1 * Letters Home From War / 12

2 * Picking Up the Pieces / 20

3 * Let Go and Live / 26

4 * My Grandparents' House / 33

5 * Seventy Times Seven / 40

LEARNING HOW TO LOVE / 47

6 * God, My Mother, and Me / 49

7 * Golden Scrapbooks of the Mind / 53

8 * The Sixteenth Life of Old Tom / 58

9 * A Gift From the Heart / 64

10 * The Waiting Parent / 71

THE POWER OF PRAYER / 78

11 * The Hour That Changed My Life / 80

12 * The Unexpected Answer / 83

13 * GrandJack Held On / 87

14 * Zigzag Faith / 92

15 * Soul on Sabbatical / 97

16 * One-Minute Prayer / 102

DISCOVERING OUR AUTHENTIC SELVES / 106

17 * I Had Money and Success; What Was Wrong? / 108

18 * The Power of Hercules / 115

19 * Love in Unexpected Places / 121

20 * Leap Into the Light / 130

21 * I'm a Recovering Perfectionist! / 138

WHAT'S REALLY IMPORTANT / 142

22 * Good-bye to the Money-God / 144

23 * The Splendid Joy of Living Simply / 148

24 * A Gift From the Woman in White / 155

25 * My Father's Last Gift / 159

26 * The Magic Word for 'God Within' / 165

Introduction

Is life turning out as you expected?

Oh.

I understand. I moved with my second husband, Bill, to a trailer on a riverbank high in the Colorado Rockies. It's a cozy mobile home and suits our needs.

Yet I confessed to a friend, "My mother told me not to play with kids who live in trailers, and now I 'are' one. It's not what I planned."

A lot of life turns out that way. Unexpected.

It occurred to me our trailer is shaped like a boat — long and narrow — so I decided to call it our river yacht. In a culture that's convinced us to wear labels on the outside and value people by the make of their cars, *yacht* seemed classier than *trailer* or *mobile home.*

"Yachts have names," observed Bill.

I smiled, thinking of *The Love Boat* in the TV series. "I'll call ours the S.S. Agape."

A-ga-pe. From the Greek, meaning God's love for humankind — and the spiritual love of one person for another.

A few days later, Bill brought me a gift: a handcrafted wooden sign that read "The S.S. Agape." We hung it on the front of our sunshine-yellow trailer, er, yacht. A neighbor came by. Puzzled, he asked, "What's that mean, the S.S. A-*gape*?"

A-gape. Well, I've often *gaped* at what's happened in my life.

I grew up wedded to a middle-class image and middle-class values. To the way things "should" be. "Do what is expected." "Learn to fit in." "Be successful." I carried pictures in my head of how my life *should* be.

None of the pictures included my river yacht.

It's as if we start out making bargains with God. Some people prefer to call it their expectation of life; but it's all the same. I've never known anyone to say, "I expect to get divorced, become seriously ill, have a child die, and lose all my money." Yet I know someone in Kansas City to whom all of those things happened.

My bargain with God was simple: I'd like to live the American Dream, please. My parents — and our culture — had raised me to expect it. Aren't we entitled?

It's like a "Peanuts" cartoon I clipped and hung behind my desk. Lucy, looking woebegone, sits with her chin in her hands. Charlie Brown comes along saying, "Cheer up, Lucy. Life has its ups and downs." Lucy, jumping to her feet, arms akimbo, replies, "But why? Why should life have ups and *downs*? Why can't it have ups — and upper ups?"

Oh, I liked that cartoon! "I'm searching for the Land of the Upper Ups," I announced, and my friends laughed, not realizing how serious I was. Surely it was here someplace. Had I mislaid it? Now I see that I looked in all the wrong places. Like the "purloined letter" in Poe's famous short story, it was right in front of me all along. I just didn't recognize it.

It's taken me years and years to understand that "the peace surpassing all understanding" *is* the Land of the Upper Ups — but it doesn't mean you get everything you ask for, or that life becomes easy, or that bad things stop happening to good people.

It does mean that God is in our corner, and we have all the grace we need to deal with life's unexpected happenings. It means God answers our prayers — only not as we expect, exactly. It's a lifelong journey to accept this fundamental truth: that we grow psychologically and spiritually only to the extent that we are willing to give up our childish bargains with God. Or life.

As long as we cling to *our* pictures of what should be, as long as we listen only to our childhood messages, we'll miss life's exciting, fulfilling reality. We won't see that prayers get answered in a way that propels us forward, out of our comfort zones, into strange lands. We're each called to be Abraham.

M. Scott Peck in *The Road Less Traveled* says we are all afflicted with laziness: We don't want to rewrite our psychological maps. It's comfortable to stay in places we know, even if those places hurt.

That's why people stay in abusive relationships. That's why we cling to jobs we hate. That's why we leave therapy as soon as we discover it's no quick fix and that the price of wholeness is the pain of moving through self-delusion into truth.

In this book you'll read some of my experiences and those of people I love. Each of us went looking for the Land of the Upper Ups, and found, instead, God's unexpected answer. You'll read about crises, big and small, because the Chinese tell us that "crisis" is just another word for "opportunity."

This is a book for sharing. Like you, I'm on the journey. If I had all the answers, would I still stumble occasionally when I tell someone I live in a trailer, er, yacht?

Growing Through Loss

Save me, O Lord, from any more <u>growing</u> experiences.

Dr. Richard Sweetland
CLINICAL PSYCHOLOGIST

Have you ever felt the aching pain of loss?

"No loss is unimportant," said a minister-friend of mine. In her book *A Time to Grieve*, Bertha Simos, DSW, agrees. Loss, says Dr. Simos, is an integral part of the human condition. None of us escapes. Yet we can become so afraid of loss that we live in perpetual fear, unwilling to risk or to enjoy the present moment. It's like the bumper sticker I saw: "Nothing ventured . . . nothing lost."

In my twenties, I was terrified of loss, yet at the same time, I thought I was impervious to it. Experts call it "the-truck-will-hit-the-other-guy syndrome."

I'm not sure we can ever prepare for loss, but the worst way is to visualize and worry about it. The best way is to rejoice in life's small, precious moments.

When I asked my ninety-one-year-old father-in-law why he was so healthy at his age, he smiled and replied, "Because I have faith in the unknown."

Yes! We're called on to trust — to believe that God will not abandon us, and that we'll find the grace to cope, no matter what happens.

In the following stories, you'll see God's grace in action during loss. And out of loss, you'll see there comes a gift — a capacity for growth that we might otherwise never discover.

1
Letters Home From War

In the early sixties, I sat at dinner one night with my husband, John, talking about the future. He'd graduated from the Naval Academy four years earlier and we'd married the year after that. What did our future hold? we wondered.

John whipped out a piece of paper and began listing his expected duty stations for the next thirty years, ending with Admiral. So this is our life, I thought.

But neither of us planned on the Vietnam war. In 1968, John was assigned to the aircraft carrier U.S.S. Bon Homme Richard off the coast of Vietnam. He was not only a Navy fighter pilot but also a husband and father, and his letters home showed the tugs he felt from those opposing roles.

31 January ● Dearest Barb: It was sad watching you and the children drive out of sight as the carrier pulled out of the harbor. Three years of shore duty were wonderful. The children's characters have really taken shape. I know them so much better now, and that makes leaving so much more difficult.

19 February ● My birthday. Does thirty-four sound old? It used to, and I think it still does. When I went down to the Ready Room, I found a large birthday cake, and when I went up to man my aircraft, I found "Happy Birthday" written on the fuselage. We've got a good crew. I like them, and they know it.

Tomorrow is your birthday, but you don't age. You're as attractive as you were when you were seventeen years old — only now, more exciting. As I write these words, I'm thinking of you and how you act, sound, feel, smell. I'm so in love with you, Barb.

25 February ● The time has come. Tomorrow we'll be on the line and I'm on the flight schedule. I feel like it was before an exam and I'm not prepared. Nervous as a cat. You can't imagine our schedule. My days start at 5:30 A.M. and go to 6:00 P.M. without a break. We then must share Condition I Air Defense (CAP) all night. (You sit in your aircraft ready to go. Two-hour watches per pilot.) Then we start again the next morning — for twenty-eight days straight or until we leave the line. I admit I'm scared of the thought of getting shot at.

27 February ● My first combat hop involved climbing through the clouds and heading for a target, only to find it was too far away. The problem then became one of landing back aboard in horrible weather. Windy, low ceilings.

A tragic loss today of one of our helicopters and crew. I played guitar with those pilots only last week.

5 March ● You can't imagine what lousy weather we've been flying in. The men are fatigued and walking around in a daze.

I'm glad the children like my letters to them. I think it's better if they have a tangible communication from Daddy rather than just a word passed via you. I can just picture Andrew saying you "lost Daddy." Poor little guy. He can't know why the normal order of things is disturbed. I'm not sure I know, myself.

10 March ● I'm back from a strike. It was a success. We (four planes) were the fighter cover and had to orbit inland to fend off MiGs, but the twelve minutes we spent over North Vietnam seemed like ten years. My mouth was so dry. What a beautiful sight the sea is when you've crossed the coastline on the way back to the ship.

12 March ● I'm sitting in the cockpit of an aircraft at 1:20 A.M. Condition I CAP. It's a lovely evening. The sea is calm and the only sound is the low whir of the gyros in my cockpit. Just now, I saw a falling star. It seems almost out of the question that I could go flying at a moment's notice.

I'm rambling on, Barb. Sort of mentally chatting with you. I can't think of anything substantial or joyous without thinking of you. I can't think of a most exquisite love without thinking of you.

16 March ● By the time you get this letter you will undoubtedly have heard of the loss of LTJG Don S. yesterday. Possibly he took an enemy hit, but visibility was poor. He may have just flown into the water. Don had been in the squadron a scant nine days.

23 April ● Operations back to a steady pace. Fresh water is low. No showers allowed. After a sweaty day of flight ops, means lots of deodorant and after-shave lotion.

24 April ● The dangers of this business hit home today. They bagged another of our squadron pilots. A parachute was seen, so he is probably alive. I'm scheduled for a strike tomorrow. I shudder to think of capture. Please pray that I'll have the presence of mind to do my job properly and with honor.

3 May ● Going on a big one again tomorrow. Things are hot out here now. It looks as if the war has escalated, but you probably have a better overall picture than we do.

Our airplanes aren't holding up at all, and we can't get parts. It's a frustrating business. My schedule has become disjointed. Up at 3:15 A.M. Fly two hops. Sleep at 2:00 P.M. Up at 5:00 P.M. Condition I CAP from seven till midnight. Up again at 6:00 A.M. And so it goes. And it's *hot*.

6 May ● Waiting to go on a big strike the past two days, but weather has prohibited. Still, life isn't boring — last night one of our aircraft caught fire on the flight deck. A sad note: This morning an enlisted man walked into a propeller. It was pretty messy. The damn flight deck continues to be a hazard, and the long hours don't help crew alertness. I hate accidents of that type. Here's a guy who is doing a difficult job — for peanuts — and putting up with long separations and lousy living conditions and he winds up dead.

After the pressure of this air war, I know what a treasure the serenity of the family is. I long to feel the children's arms around me, to play the role of the lion with his cubs. Tears come to my eyes when I think how I want to be with my children, playing with them, explaining things to them, trying to give them some of myself. And then to think of you, my greatest asset. You've flooded my life with goodness. You are the source of all that's dear to me.

14 May ● We're now steaming full speed toward Yankee station (line combat), two days early. Could this be escalation? Stay tuned.

19 May ● A bad day for us. The opposition was the worst ever, they say. Two pilots are reported missing. A good chance they were captured. I hope so. As one man put it yesterday, "You can't come back from the dead, but you might make it out of prison camp."

20 May ● I am scheduled for the next strike . . . a tough one . . . target is in downtown Hanoi. I don't mind telling you I'm scared. I hope I can get this out of my system prior to launch. (I will, of course.) By the time you receive this letter, the strike will be history.

21 May ● I went to Mass this morning. We brief for the big strike at noon. Before the strike, Barb, it's important for me to tell you again how much I love you. Without you, my life would be shallow and empty.

. . . I am happy to be continuing this letter. The strike was a success and we got everyone back, which is the most important thing. I have done difficult things in my life, but that has got to be the roughest. I had to fly right over downtown Hanoi. They shot everything in the book at us, and I'll bet I perspired five gallons of water.

31 May ● Today was glorious in one way. Received a wonderful photograph of you and the children. Barb, I can't tell you not to worry or not to be afraid. All I can say is, I hope it's God's will that I return to you in August as scheduled. There is nothing I want more than to go on the camping trip that Barty [John, Jr.] keeps talking about.

2 June ● Thanks for your letter with Barty's tooth in it! I wish I could hear Bart laugh right now. He has such an infectious laugh. I love him so. Tell Sony [Allison's nickname] that I love my little girl very much. And Andrew, too.

3 June ● I am sad to report that Dave W. was lost at sea early this morning. Search is still in progress. He took off at 2:30 A.M., and that was the last contact. In the face of war, one tends to forget the hazards of flying off a carrier.

Hope you're saying some prayers. My emotions are a mix of self-pity, fear, pride, sadness, anger. I wonder if I have courage — and if I do, what is it all worth? Of course, we must maintain the outward appearance of fearless composure.

4 June ● We are inventorying and packing Dave's things. What a depressing job. I liked Dave better than anyone else in the squadron. I still can't get used to the idea that he's gone. P.S. Our flight surgeon just stopped in to give me a cigar. His wife gave birth to a girl. I told him, news of a *birth* is welcome, indeed.

6 June ● Tomorrow I will have been commissioned for ten years, and next week we will have been married nine years. Nine wonderful years to a girl who makes me feel nine feet tall and who has borne me three beautiful children. Without you, my darling, I'd be like an autumn leaf — dry and lifeless. With you loving me, spring is always in the offing.

Again, sad news. Yesterday we lost a photo pilot. Just two days earlier, he and I had made the same run together. They were shooting like mad. Yesterday, they got lucky. Damn war. So depressing.

9 June ● Dear Bart: How are you, son? I sure enjoyed the tape recording of you, Mommy, Sony, and Andrew. And I enjoyed your joke, too . . .

Dear Sony: I enjoy getting letters from you. Help your mother and be a good big sister to your brothers. Love, "Daddy-O."

12 June ● A quiet Sunday. Only two big air strikes. John M. got shot down east of Haiphong but was picked up. You can't imagine the anxiety of waiting for the helo to get him. Alfred Hitchcock couldn't have duplicated the suspense. Yes sir, a drama a day.

A new pilot came aboard yesterday — an ensign. Poor kid was in the Ready Room when we got back from the Hanoi raid. Must have been something to see all these pilots come in soaked in their sweat, hair askew, with dry mouths, adrenalin still up, and breathing heavy. That's a hell of a way to meet the squadron!

I'm looking at the beautiful pictures you sent me of the children. I see such *hope* in their eyes. I want so much to hold them in my arms, Barb. I want to be there to influence my children, to bring out their good qualities. What greater success can a father ask?

14 June ● Awards were given out today, and I got my first air medal. The award that would please me most would be a trip back home. Four more days of this line period. The ship expects to arrive in San Diego in August. That means our big camping trip is set for September.

27 June ● Tomorrow starts our last line period. Thirty-two more days of combat . . . I want to hold you in my arms, taste the sweetness of your lips, feel the softness of your cheek next to mine, make love to you. How deeply I love you, darling.

3 July ● Tomorrow is the 4th of July. There's a theory that the North Viets are saving all their SAMs for tomorrow.

I'm on the first launch. Three strikes a day until further notice. I don't think the idea of July 4th has ever had so much meaning for me as it does now.

21 July ● Big day for VF-24. Bob Kirkwood (my roommate) and Red Isaacks (XO) both shot down MiGs this morning. Good guys win, too.

25 July ● Three more days till we leave the line.

29 July ● I can't believe this has happened. This morning at 7:00 I was thinking happy thoughts. Combat flying was over. Bob and I congratulated each other on having conducted ourselves honorably and with excellence. At 11:00, we got word of a fire on the aircraft carrier *Forrestal*. We steamed full speed to give assistance. Smoke was billowing out of her stern section, and the charred remnants of some aircraft were visible on the flight deck. At least twenty people killed and a lot more injured.

How does it affect us? We're extended on the line for an indefinite period.

31 August ● My darling John: I love you. They're trying to tell me you're dead. You can't be — we have so much to do together. Remember our camping trip? Remember how we joke and laugh together?

Oh, John, I love you — John, you can't be dead . . .

That note was scrawled in the handwriting of a young woman who thought she knew exactly how her life would unfold.

Years would pass before I grew beyond my soul-searing disbelief and anger at God — before I could see that, yes, even John's death held an answer.

On Memorial Day 1982, I felt a sudden impulse to go down to our basement. I had married again by this time, but I still had my dusty box of John's letters, appropriately tied in pink yarn.

I began to read them and then, as if possessed, to excerpt them, working all day and night, until at 5:00 A.M., tired but satisfied, I finished. I mailed my manuscript to *Reader's Digest*.

The *Digest* published John's letters in its October 1982 issue; the same month and year the Vietnam War Memorial was unveiled in Washington, D.C. Phone calls and letters poured in, for John's voice, fifteen years after his death, was one of the first to speak for others who fought in our "unpopular war."

2
Picking Up the Pieces

In the bleak year that followed John's death, I felt as if I'd plunged down some enormous black hole. I missed little things the most. The way John and I touched toes at night as we slept. Our Saturday ritual of shopping together, always winding up at the ice-cream store. The silly game he played with our three kids: "Everybody who loves Mommy, raise your right hand . . . wiggle your left ear . . . blink your middle eye . . . What? No middle eye?" The kids always got a kick out of that one.

Sometimes, as I folded clothes or brought in groceries — all the usual tasks that had to go on — I felt like a vase that I remembered from my grandmother's house. Something had struck it, shooting hairline cracks all through it. From a distance, it still looked whole, but one day, before our eyes, it simply collapsed and fell into pieces.

Would that happen to me? I wondered. I prayed for God's help, but it was so hard to hold myself together without John.

My parents missed John, too. And they worried about me. "Why don't you go back to school?" suggested my mother, about eight months after John died. "I'll help with the kids."

I liked her idea. Now that I was head of my small family, I knew I'd soon need a job. A college degree would help. I signed up at once for three courses. It was exciting to be one of the students who poured across the sprawling campus each morning, to overhear ideas argued back and forth as students hurried past me, to feel part of something again.

Quickly I decided that my most stimulating class was taught by Alan Peppard (not his real name), a young professor with a doctorate from Berkeley.

One October morning, between classes, I bumped into him in the student union.

"Join me for coffee," he invited with a friendly smile.

I was delighted and followed him eagerly through the noisy crush of people. He wasn't a tall man, but he had a freewheeling, sure-of-himself sort of walk. In class he would stride back and forth, pointing his finger. "You! In the second row. What do you think?" Anything to get us involved in a subject he obviously adored: Romantic English literature.

"You turned in a good paper last week," he said, as we found a table. I blushed like a teenager. Alan — though I thought of him then as Dr. Peppard — was known to be a very tough grader.

He asked me about myself and soon, ignoring the banging of trays and high-pitched student voices all around us, I began telling him about John, and the plane crash, and how I hoped to earn my bachelor's, maybe even my master's, degree.

Alan, I learned, was a never-married bachelor of thirty-five. He liked classical music (so did I) and the theater and sailing. Especially sailing. He owned his own sailboat.

"There's something about the freedom — the solitude you find on the water. Know what I mean?" I had never sailed, but I nodded.

A few weeks later Alan stopped me after class and held out two tickets to the symphony. The next week he asked me if I'd like to go sailing. Later he invited me to a faculty party.

"Is Alan your boyfriend?" Barty, my eight-year-old son, asked as he watched me get ready for the party.

"Would you mind if he was?"

He glanced at his brother and sister before replying, "No, it's okay."

I breathed a sigh of relief at his answer. The kids ran out to play while I happily sprayed on perfume.

All that fall, Alan and I saw each other. On Christmas Day he helped Barty balance on his new two-wheeler. He snapped toy parts together for six-year-old Andy and admired ten-year-old Sony's new doll. He even listened patiently as my father went on and on about football. When we gathered around our holiday table, I prayed, with true gratitude, "Thank you, Lord, for bringing Alan into my life."

One week later, on New Year's Eve, Alan said softly, "Barbara, I love you." And then, a moment later, "Hey, why the tears?"

I couldn't answer. It seemed like such a miracle to be loved again. Yet I heard Alan's words with the tremulous awareness that to accept them — to return them — made me vulnerable again. Car accidents happen, too. What if I lost Alan as I had lost John?

What a silly, morbid thought!

"I love you," I finally said to Alan.

The winter passed, and we continued to attend concerts, go to parties, share activities and ideas. Alan and the children seemed comfortable together. We set our wedding date for June.

In May, when Alan arrived one evening, I brought out a sample of the wedding invitations I'd chosen. "How do you like it?" I asked, sliding next to him on the couch. "I've ordered two hundred."

His silent stare, as he examined the engraved stationery, didn't disturb me. By now I was used to Alan's slow, thoughtful habit of contemplation. As he often reminded me, he liked to consider everything carefully.

"Just four more weeks and we'll be a family," I said, squeezing his arm. "Well, how do you like it?"

He cleared his throat, and suddenly I was aware of the agitation that showed in his eyes.

"Alan, is something wrong?"

He looked away from me. When he finally spoke, his voice sounded hollow. And what he said seemed incomprehensible. I stared at him. Stupidly. I must have heard wrong.

"I can't go through with it, Barbara," he said again. "I'm sorry. I can't marry you."

My ears buzzed. Something inside me seemed to crack, like my grandmother's vase.

"I — I wanted to want to marry you," Alan stammered, then blurted: "I tried, I really did! But I've been independent for so long. I like my freedom. I'm just not ready for a family. Can you understand?"

From far away I heard the front door bang open and then shut again, as if the kids had sensed something terrible was going on and retreated.

"Please try to understand," he repeated. But all I understood was the dreadful emptiness of yet another loss.

In the days and weeks that followed, I felt as bereft as I had after John died. And angry.

I struggled along with classes — just barely. But I seemed to be sleepwalking. From what I saw of Alan, though — and now it was little — he seemed to be carrying on with his *independent life* just fine.

One morning, as I reached for a juice glass, something inside of me exploded. "It's not fair!" I screamed out loud and threw the glass as hard as I could. It careened off the wall and shattered noisily against the kitchen floor. I stood, looking down. My life seemed as shattered as the bits of jagged glass strewn across my kitchen floor.

That summer, instead of our usual lively trips to the beach, I found myself lying across my bed, staring into space.

My mother picked up the kids for swimming lessons and day camp. "You've got to snap out of this," she urged.

But I couldn't shake my lethargy. As the golden summer days went on, I stayed in a dark depression.

"What's wrong, Mommy?" asked Barty.

"Nothing, honey," I said, trying to sound cheerful. But the effort was more than I could manage.

August came and with it the deadline for university enrollment. I ignored it. But my parents didn't. My mother, especially, kept after me.

"You're too close to graduation to quit now," she insisted.

Reluctantly, I agreed. The next day, I drove to the campus to register. After parking, I headed across the familiar green quadrangle toward the college gymnasium where I knew students would be milling noisily around the sign-up tables.

Suddenly, I saw Alan, striding across the campus in my direction! I couldn't face him. It still hurt too much. In panic, I darted into the first doorway I saw — and found myself inside the college chapel.

I had probably passed the small stone chapel hundreds of times but had never gone inside. It was empty. Thick walls muffled the college clamor outside. Wooden pews faced an altar that was bare. But behind the altar was a stained-glass window through which light flooded the chapel. I slid into one of the pews.

To some, the chapel might have held a quiet, dusty peace. All I felt was an unpleasant queasiness, as if I were in an elevator that had dropped too suddenly.

My throat clogged and I began to cry. "I'm not going to make it," I said to the empty air. Dust motes danced in the silence. I bowed my head in prayer. And as I sat in the quiet, something made me lift my head — and look directly at the stained-glass window.

It dominated the little chapel. Two stories high, it showed God's finger reaching toward man's in a depiction of Michelangelo's famed painting. A mosaic of colored glass chips formed a rose-and-lavender border.

I suddenly had the feeling that God was reaching down to touch me at this very moment. Slowly it dawned on me. This window — this beautiful, whole window — was formed from hundreds of tiny pieces of broken, shattered glass! If those fragments could be shaped into a wonderful, whole pattern, couldn't God do the same with the shattered pieces of my life?

I caught my breath.

As clearly as if I heard the words aloud, a voice spoke inside me: *Pick up the pieces, Barbara. Make something of them. Something beautiful.*

I stared, openmouthed, at the stained-glass mosaic. Suddenly, for one brief, luminous instant, I seemed to see in my future a kaleidoscope of possibilities. Mother! Graduate! Working woman! And, yes, perhaps even wife again. Successful! Happy!

Then the moment was gone. Only the stained-glass window remained, with August sunlight slanting through it. I sat for a long time, staring at it and at all the bits of broken glass that had created it.

Something in me changed after that day. I saw that marriage to Alan was not the only way to rebuild my life. Depression gave way to a sense of acceptance, and eventually, to an eagerness to go on. I finished my undergraduate studies and enrolled in graduate school.

"Mommy," said Barty one day, sliding his small hand into mine, "are you happy again?"

Into my mind flashed the chapel window. I smiled and squeezed Barty's hand as I replied, "Why, yes, honey, I believe I am."

3
Let Go and Live

After John died, I spent a year in which, like pulling out threads in some beautiful tapestry, I let go, thread by thread, of all that mattered to me.

Even my faith in God was shaken. I'd always thought bad things wouldn't happen to *me*. I was a good person and God would protect me. John's death turned my religious assumptions topsy-turvy.

Now, many years later, I know that letting go is something all of us experience, and it doesn't require death. We leave neighborhoods we know and love. We marry and raise families, and our children leave home. We get transferred or lose jobs. Our parents die, and so does the dog.

In every new experience, happy or sad, there's a need to let go of what *was*. Until we do, we can't appreciate what *is*. We need to let go of people and situations, and also of outgrown values and expectations.

My friend Jennifer was a nun for fifteen years before she decided to leave the convent. She told me, "God calls on us to grow and become all that we can be. If you're no longer growing in your present environment, you need to ask: Am I called to leave?"

But "leaving" and "letting go" aren't easy.

I remember when my daughter, Sony, left for college. I took a long look at her lemon-yellow walls and ruffled bedspread and said, "I think I'll turn this room into a study."

"No!" cried Sony. "I need my bedroom!" I hid a smile. She really meant, "I'm not ready to let go of my childhood home." So we left her room alone. By spring semester of her senior year, she casually remarked, "Oh, by the way, Mom, if you want to do something with my bedroom, go ahead. I don't need it anymore." In her own time and in her own way, Sony had let go.

It's important to allow enough time to say good-bye.

Good-byes are part of every transition and there are no shortcuts. It's in this period we may feel dislocated, cut adrift, angry, even "crazy."

I still remember something Annie said. She and I shared several classes when I went back to college after John died. "One thing about death," she said slowly, "it's a clean stroke of the knife. I'm getting divorced, and divorce is a *hacking* away." We sat in the sun, yet I shivered. There are other experiences that hack away at us — a bad work environment, a chronic illness, an alcoholic spouse, to name just three. The bloody feeling of *being hacked at* is part of our good-bye process; it takes faith to believe that the hacking will end. It will.

In the years since John died, we've adopted a saying in our family: "We shouldn't wallow in self-pity. But sometimes it's okay to swish our feet a little." It's our way of acknowledging that when changes come or disappointments happen, everyone can use some "feel-bad" time before moving on. It's all part of saying good-bye. The point is not to *wallow*.

It helps to seek support, too, when you're letting go. My good friend Marna Lahodney wrote to friends around the globe when her cancer metastasized. "I need you," she said, simply. "I need you to pray for me and call me and send me letters and let me know you love me." Marna lived, joyously and nearly pain-free, a year longer than her doctors expected. I'm convinced that the support she asked for and received helped extend her life.

Some people are afraid to ask for support, afraid to seem "weak" or to let people know they hurt. But *all* of us need support at some time in our lives.

When John died, support groups didn't exist. I felt so alone as I tried to deal with my grief. There weren't even books available. Now, you can find support for almost every calamity. Survivors After Suicide, Widowed Persons, Alcoholics Anonymous, Parkinson Support Groups . . . the list goes on and on. Experts have found that peer support *works*, sometimes more effectively than professional counseling.

I discovered other ways to find support, and they may also help you when you've experienced a terrible loss or even when you're simply feeling blue: Try turning to nature. Walk on the beach, hike in the mountains, or simply gaze at a star-studded night sky. Nature's grandeur — that sense of being part of something larger than ourselves — can bring unexpected peace and help repair or soften the disappointments in our lives.

Society's rituals give public support to life's passage and the letting-go process. That's why we hold Bar Mitzvahs, confirmations, weddings, funerals. On New Year's Eve, the Unity church in West Palm Beach, Florida, has a Burning Bowl ceremony. Church members examine their lives and write down what they'll let go of in the coming year. Their papers are dropped into a fire that burns in a Grecian urn, symbolizing the completeness of their release. Afterward, each person writes a "letter to God" affirming goals for the coming year. Why not create a private "letting go" ritual — perhaps your own Burning Bowl ceremony?

In the year after John died, I tried to present a strong face to the world, and many people admiringly said, "Barbara, you're so brave." But at home, after I tended to my children's basic needs, I disappeared into my bedroom, shut the door, and lay across my bed, grieving.

At that point in my life, I hadn't accepted my new reality, and until I did, I couldn't move on. It's easy to get *stuck*.

Bill Bowle (a pseudonym) is a case in point. I learned about Bill a few years ago. Three weeks after his wedding, the twenty-one-year-old bridegroom suffered a broken neck that left him a quadriplegic. But more than a wheelchair imprisoned

Bill — alcohol and prescription drugs left him, as he told me later, "in a nine-year blackout." He and his wife divorced. Finally, AA — Alcoholics Anonymous — helped Bill get in touch with reality, accept that he would not walk again, and release the resentment he'd hidden from himself. He married again, got a college degree, and became a leader in networking groups for the disabled.

Once we accept what *is* and stop yearning for what *might have been*, we can make a good life. Though short-term denial is nature's way of shielding us from what we cannot yet bear, it's important to avoid getting *stuck*.

Sometimes, we get stuck in an outgrown message. When she was growing up in Connecticut, my good friend Carol heard from her widowed mother: "Your sister is brilliant. Your brother's a leader. You're cute and athletic but scatterbrained." When Carol wanted to major in English literature in college, her mother said, "Too intellectual for you, dear. Major in P.E." So Carol became a physical-education teacher. She was fifty years old when she decided to prove her mother wrong. She enrolled at our state University in English lit and made straight A's; now she's earning her doctorate.

Emotions Anonymous, a self-help group based on AA's twelve-step program, suggests saying this: "Just for today . . . I will adjust myself to what *is*. I will accept my family, my friends, my business, my circumstances *as they come*."

It's also important to leave blame behind. Many losses prompt unjustified feelings of guilt and self-blame. My middle child, Barty, buried his sorrow about his father's death behind a wall of anger. He started getting in trouble at school, at home, and in the neighborhood. I blamed myself for not being able to help my son. When I looked in the mirror, all I saw was a parent who wasn't good enough.

Well, I *had* made mistakes. But eventually time and some counseling taught me to see that I'd done my best. I came to understand that I could help my son more if I let go of my own disabling guilt. When I was able to do that, Barty began letting go of his anger.

There's a big difference between regret, which is healthy, and guilt, which is not. Regret lets you love yourself, put your mistake behind you, and go on.

Sometimes, we take on guilt that isn't even ours. Rape victims may express guilt or shame as a subconscious way to fend off the awful helplessness they experienced. Guilt at least gives an illusion to the victim that she had some control. ("It must have been my fault . . .")

Men, especially, blame themselves for the act of grieving, as if they're being weak. It helps to lower your personal demands on yourself following a loss. Remember, feelings of incompetence and dependency during grief are natural — and temporary.

It helps lighten our sorrow when we help others. A lot of great causes have been launched by those who grieve.

Candy Lightner started Mothers Against Drunk Driving (MADD) after her daughter Cari was killed by a drunken driver. After six-year-old Adam Walsh was kidnapped and murdered, his father, John, brought hope to many other parents by successfully lobbying for national legislation to help find missing children. Sarah Brady's gun control bill is a response to her husband's injury in the attack on President Reagan.

In my city, sociology professor Ed Chasteen was diagnosed with multiple sclerosis and fell into a deep depression. Then he discovered he could still bicycle and decided to bicycle — penniless — across the country. He would prove how generous people can be and also raise funds for MS. With empty pockets, he bicycled from one corner of the country to the other — Orlando, Florida, to Seattle, Washington — raising funds and people's consciousness along the way.

Doing something for others, however, doesn't have to be so ambitious. Just after John died, when my shoulders still ached with grief, I took my three children to the beach. Gulls wheeled overhead. Ours were the first footprints in the sand. The children ran ahead, their voices shrill as they piped, "Mommy, run! Run with us!" So I ran after them, and when I caught them, we collapsed in the sand, laughing, happy to be together because we knew we were all suffering the same deep loss. In that small act of mothering, in the joy of reaching out, I forgot how sad I was. For a wonderful moment, I let go of my grief.

In every experience, there is an "unexpected answer." Dr. Joseph Hyland, a psychiatrist at Menninger, the mental-health facility in Topeka, Kansas, told me that the people who do best after catastrophic change are those who can perceive the good in what is left of their lives.

I drove my friend Carolyn, thirty-two, to the dentist to have all her teeth pulled. She coped with her loss by eventually congratulating herself on having gained a prettier smile with dentures.

A man I know spent ten years developing an idea he felt would revolutionize a segment of the food industry. But he ran out of money and had to give up. At age fifty, in debt, he had nothing to show for his work. How did he describe himself? "Why, I'm just a late bloomer. Watch what happens in the next ten years!" Once he realized he had done everything he could with his idea, he let go of his failure and never looked back. "Nothing is ever lost," he told me. "What I learned I'll put to use somewhere else."

Gerald Jampolsky, M.D., founder of The Center for Attitudinal Healing, in Tiburon, California, has hung in his home a collection of photographs he's taken of empty hands. Says Dr. Jampolsky, who authored *Love Means Letting Go of Fear*, "Peace of mind means keeping your hand open by not holding on to what is past. It's only when you open your hand to let go that you also open it to receive."

I would never have chosen to lose my husband so young, yet his death taught me that I had strengths I was unaware of. With widowhood came the surfacing of an inner self I had never explored before. I've done more with my life than I otherwise might have, because change and growth were thrust upon me.

I've learned, though it took a few years, that pain is a natural part of living. When I let go of my demands for how I thought my world should be, I found one of the greatest gifts of all: I found myself.

4
My Grandparents' House

The old house seemed comfortable with itself, as it quietly dozed in the melancholy twilight of Indian summer. A proper Victorian, it spread out its wide front porch like an ample lap.

I stood on the sidewalk, as if to glimpse again that sturdy little girl with brown bangs who used to run across the porch, calling to her grandparents, "I'm here! Granny! Granddad! I'm here!"

But no answering voice called back, in pretended astonishment, "Why, Barbara Helen, is that really you? Hurry! Come, give me a hug."

No feet in scuffed oxfords clattered across the porch. No laughter or girlish squeals. The house of my childhood dozed silently in the October afternoon, no longer mine.

My cheeks ached with the pressure of unshed tears. I grieved as if someone dear had died.

Looking back, I now realize that we accept whatever our childhoods bring us.

I was a child of the 1940s, an era when kids ran barefoot in small towns and rode safely alone on subways in cities. Yet it wasn't a tranquil time; newspapers and radio blared the war news.

I was only six, so to me the war meant fun things like squishing the plastic bag to spread the yellow in the oleo, and not-such-fun things like having makeshift toys because of rationing.

The war made me sad because my daddy, tall and mustached, in officer's khakis, left us to go overseas. But it

33

made me *happy*, too, because my mother, brother, and I moved home to Durango, Colorado, to live in my grandparents' big old house.

Mountain-ringed Durango was a child's dream. I could run down to Woolworth's on Main Street all by myself. On summer Saturdays, I went fishing with my granddad, bumping along dusty dirt roads in his old Ford with the running boards. In his barn behind the house, fragrant with age, I discovered treasures: old bottle caps and Mason jars, piles of *National Geographic*s, wooden toys left from an earlier generation.

My grandmother's face felt soft as a doeskin glove, and wrinkles etched her skin like the fine lines on sterling silver. I loved to rub my cheek against hers. We sat in her rocker at night, while she read me stories like *Black Beauty*.

I couldn't name it then, but years later I knew the word I felt was *secure*; in my grandparents' house I felt secure and loved, and I would never know such security again. When the war ended, Daddy came home and we became an Army family. Right away, we moved.

"Now remember, Barbara Helen, to make a friend you have—"

"I know, I know," I interrupted. " 'To make a friend you have to *be* a friend.' "

My mother smiled. "That's right. Now go on. Meet the new kids." She brushed back her curly hair, leaving a streak of dirt on one cheek, and plunged her hands into another cardboard packing box.

"The other kids aren't new; I am," I muttered. But my mother, engrossed in unwrapping dishes, didn't seem to hear — or perhaps pretended she hadn't.

The warm California sunshine seemed strange. In New Jersey, where we'd lived until a week ago, I'd been walking through snow. Here kids were running in shorts. As I drew closer, dawdling my way down the sidewalk, they stopped and stared. I felt butterflies inside. "Just be a friend, be a friend, be a friend," I whispered as a "mantra" to myself. But it was never that simple.

I was in fourth grade now, and this was our twelfth move. In the Army you were supposed to cope when orders came. "Army brats" like me learned to shrug and pack. The year before, in third grade, I'd gone to three schools.

I was a shy girl, and secretly hated the ritual I was about to start: putting on a smile, forcing out the words "Hi, I'm Barbara." Sometimes I didn't bother. In Spokane the year before, I'd read library books. We were only there for three months and no one seemed to care about getting to know me. I heard my mother say to a friend, "Barbara Helen is such a good reader. I'm proud of her!"

Once I tried to explain how hard it was to say good-bye so often, but Mom's face got a peculiar crimped expression, as if her tooth ached, so I didn't bring the subject up again.

I loved our summer visits to Durango. As my father turned the corner into town, excitement bubbled like soda-pop fizz. I'd watch intently and hold my breath. There it was! My grandparents' house, and yes, it looked the same! My oxfords clattered across the wide front porch. Into the kitchen I ran for Granny's hug, her soft, soft cheek rubbing mine.

Our visits always seemed too short. It was easy to pick up again with the kids I'd gone to school with while Daddy was away in the war. In Durango, I didn't have to make new friends; I had that precious commodity: *old* friends.

"Barbara," said my mother, her voice tense, "walk beside me, please, and don't run off." I was nine. It was November 1949, and we had walked into a crowded street in Shanghai,

China, pungent with odors of dung and humanity. The American armed forces, which included my father, had been ordered to China to support Chiang Kai-shek in China's civil war. But Mao Tse-tung's guerrillas were winning. Now American and European military dependents were fleeing the danger.

My mother's tight voice showed her fear, but I wasn't worried about the war. I was angry. The Girl Scout leader had told me I couldn't join her troop because I was younger than my classmates — too young by Girl Scout standards. *Not fair!* I thought, kicking a pebble in the crowded street. I seethed at the unfairness of grown-ups.

We left China on a ship jam-packed with women and children, bound for Japan. "I'll join you when I can," promised my father, running his fingers through my mother's bouncy curls. "Maybe by Christmas."

"Come soon," Mom whispered, nuzzling his cheek. "And stay safe."

It never occurred to my brother or me that Daddy might be in danger. I just wanted to get settled after six weeks spent in a Shanghai hotel room.

But we spent Christmas that year in another hotel room, this one in Yokohama, just south of Tokyo. We had a spindly sprig of pine in our room that my mother said solemnly was just as good as a big Christmas tree, and had one gift each because you weren't allowed to buy more in the post-war Army exchange.

Daddy arrived in February and we moved to Tokyo to a real house. For the third time that year, I walked into a new classroom.

"Remember," said Mom, "to make a friend . . ."

"I know, I know," I said, and sighed resignedly.

All during Daddy's Army tour in Japan, I held a mental picture of my grandparents' house. When anyone asked where I came from, I smiled and said, "Durango." If someone looked puzzled, I quickly added, "Colorado."

We drove there as soon as our ship docked in the States two years later. I held my breath as Daddy turned our car down the familiar street. Overhead, the sky was like a brilliant blue bowl. Yellow dandelions sprouted in yards, and I happily sniffed the clear mountain air.

Then I noticed my mother squeezing her hands together, so tightly the skin had whitened. "Why, she's excited, too," I thought. It was the first time I realized that grown-ups keep touchstones, too — special places they hold on to.

There it was! Basking in the sun. The sloping roof still shaded the wide front porch, and roses climbed the red brick walls. I glimpsed the weathered barn out back. As I raced into the kitchen, the linoleum creaked in a familiar way, and I smelled my grandmother's Yardley cologne as we hugged. Her cheek felt as soft as a doeskin glove. "Barbara Helen," she beamed, "it's so good to have you home."

It didn't matter that I'd been gone two years. My friends welcomed me back, and we went fishing and swimming and hiking in the mountains. All too soon, my father announced, "Time to get going," and we left for his next duty station, this time in Montgomery, Alabama.

From Montgomery, we moved to Washington, D.C. Then my father got orders to Germany, and after that, to California. I went off to college, married John, and had a baby.

John and I visited my grandparents when Sony was a year old. As we turned down their street, I felt the familiar fizz of excitement. There it was, and it hadn't changed! I watched my little daughter toddle across the wide porch.

John and my grandfather took to each other right away. "Let's go fishing," Granddad said. I hugged him. He felt smaller than before.

Then I rubbed my cheek against my grandmother's, marveling, as always, at its softness. It was our last meeting. Eight months later, Granny died.

Now, a year later, I stood in the Indian summer twilight, looking across at their house, knowing I couldn't go inside because Granddad, telling no one, had sold it a few months after my grandmother died. The family outcry surprised and confused him. "I thought I'd save everyone trouble," he mumbled.

Without the house or my grandmother, he seemed to shrink, and now I'd come for his funeral.

I felt sad about Granddad, but losing the house left me feeling bereft. My throat tightened. I tried to hold back sobs, but they came anyway. "It's just a house!" I wept. "Just a silly old house! Why am I crying?"

Years later, I slid into the tent we'd pitched high in the Sierras. Sony, Barty, and Andy were snuggled into sleeping bags, and through the tent flap I watched flames from our campfire dancing into the night sky as a bird gave a mournful call.

"Tell us a Barbara Helen story!" said John. (Soon after Barty turned thirteen, he wanted to be called by his given name.)

I smiled. "Barbara Helen" stories were special, just for campouts like this one. "Well," I began, "one day Barbara Helen went to visit her grandparents, who lived in a big old house in the mountains of Colorado. Barbara Helen ran across the wide front porch . . ."

As I wove my story, the house glowed in my mind. My touchstone, the one unchanging part of my nomadic childhood. No wonder I loved it so much.

I wept for the house when my grandfather sold it. But when I told my first "Barbara Helen" story, the house magically reappeared, and I saw that I had never really lost it, for you never lose something you love. Why, I could even give the house to my children. In the darkness I smiled and continued: "Barbara Helen's grandmother had skin as soft as a doeskin glove . . ."

5
Seventy Times Seven

It was a hot September afternoon, Nancy Hall told me, but she shivered as she sat in the wood-paneled California courtroom, staring at the man who had killed her child in one of the most horrible ways imaginable: Seventeen-year-old Mark had burned to death, trapped inside his exploding car after it was hit.

Nancy clenched her hands, feeling nauseous. *Look at me,* she ordered inside her mind. *Look at me, and see how I hate you.* But the businessman who had collected two DWIs before he slammed into Mark's car kept his eyes on the floor.

I'll never forgive you, Nancy thought. *Never.*

Years later, when Nancy and I talked, she admitted, in a tone of quiet wonder, "Yes, I did forgive him, though I never intended to."

When I told Nancy's story to a group of friends, their reactions surprised me.

"How could she forgive him? Her child burned to death!"

"If some drunk killed my child, I'd hate him forever!"

"Drunk drivers have to be punished. Forgiving him is like excusing what he did."

I remembered Nancy's soft voice, almost sighing as she said, "I didn't do it for him, but for me. It brought me peace."

Forgiveness is one of life's hardest tasks. I was in my forties before I conceded the need to forgive my parents for yanking me from one place to another as a "military brat." I couldn't forgive, though, until I stopped stuffing my grief and acknowledged it.

And when I got fired from an ad-agency job — unfairly, I thought — I had to recognize healthy anger versus unhealthy bitterness before I could pass to forgiveness.

Hardest of all, though, was forgiving God when John died. And later, forgiving *myself* for being a less-than-perfect parent.

It's tough to forgive, even when it's something undramatic. A driver nearly runs you off the road and four hours later, you're still fuming. Or you and your spouse have a fight, and you go to bed angry, each waiting for the other to say, "I'm sorry." Or a work colleague gets the promotion you wanted — and you think, *I can't forgive him! Why should I?*

Well, one reason is your health. "I call it the two-thousand-year-old health tip," I heard a minister say. "The Bible says, 'forgive seventy times seven,' and the one who is healed is the one who forgives."

Giving up resentment is key to the twelve-step programs. Yet it's so much easier to say than to do.

I talked to Dr. Gerald Jampolsky, who's authored many books on love and healing. The doctor of medicine told me when he asks his audiences, "How many of you have *not* totally forgiven your parents for their mistakes?" seventy-five percent raise their hands. In divorced groups, thirty-five percent say they're still angry at a former spouse. Ironically, said Dr. Jampolsky, anger ties you to your ex-spouse — even if you physically marry someone else — and as long as you blame your parents for your problems, you never fully take charge of your own life.

It's hard to give up anger when we feel we're innocent victims who were wronged. Anger creates an illusion of strength while forgiveness implies weakness. And there are times when honest rage can protect you from becoming a victim again. Battered wives typically forgive their husbands after a beating, yet experts in spouse abuse agree the "honeymoon" never lasts. Rage is what gives a woman courage to escape her situation.

My friend Betty felt enraged when she learned her husband had cheated on her, even though he gave up his affair. On the positive side, her anger galvanized her to go back to work, which raised her self-esteem. She rejoined her church and started meeting with a local support group. Eventually, she realized, "I don't need my husband; I can get along on my own." That's when Betty said she made a choice. She decided her marriage had enough good in it to save, if she could give up her anger. Forgiveness came naturally then, but the process required five years.

A man I once worked with, raised by a harsh authoritarian father, couldn't forgive his father until the man was old and ill. "I saw him, finally, as a vulnerable human being, and that's when years of resentment fell away," he told me.

What helped me on my own path to forgiveness was discovering that it doesn't have to happen *between* two people. When I talked to psychologist Susan Trout, who writes and speaks about attitudinal healing, she explained: "Forgiveness is not an action you perform with another person; it's an attitude you choose — a state of being. It's not about one person being right and the other wrong, or about a sinner needing punishment. It's not even necessary to confront the other person. Forgiveness is your willingness to search for a truth that lies beyond the apparent situation."

The truth is, we come at forgiveness obliquely, just as we do happiness, after facing the reality of a situation and acknowledging our feelings.

"Getting even" is what some people substitute for forgiveness, especially after a rejection. "Don't get mad; get even" is a popular saying. But it doesn't work because getting even won't fill the emptiness inside. On the other hand if you tell yourself, "I *should* forgive because it's the right thing to do," your forgiveness won't be authentic, and won't last.

In a dramatic episode on Oprah Winfrey's talk show, a seventeen-year-old girl spoke to the man who, four years earlier, had beaten her beyond recognition and left her for dead. She needed seventeen surgeries and complete facial reconstruction. Before the TV audience, she told the man, "I don't hate you. I hate what you did to me. And I've had to learn to forgive you so I could go on with my own life." Recalling it later, Oprah said, "It was the most powerful thing I've ever seen."

True forgiveness *is* powerful. People who can't let go of their anger risk becoming bitter, emotionally stunted, or physically ill.

I searched for workable steps I could use in forgiving, and here's what I learned.

First, borrow from the twelve-step programs and examine yourself instead of the person who's wronged you. Look honestly at your own errors, and ask, "Why am I so resentful? Where do I feel most threatened? Is it my self-esteem? My physical self? My financial well-being? My need for approval from others?"

In a kindly, nonjudgmental way, inventory how you have hurt others. Be willing to make amends, and do so whenever possible. If you're wondering, "Why should I look at myself when I've been hurt by someone else?" the answer is simple: "Once we accept our own imperfections, we begin to see others as human, instead of monsters."

My friends and neighbors Harriet and Len disappeared from my life after John died. I simply didn't see them again, and it devastated me. Years later, long after I'd moved from the neighborhood, I clung to my anger. Then, in 1989, I let a good friend down when she was terminally ill, and I saw that Harriet, Len, and I had all lacked courage. If I forgave myself, I had to forgive them, and I did.

Forgiveness is seldom a single act. *Allow yourself time to process your pain and anger*, but try to vent your anger in a healthy way, without damaging yourself or someone else. You might go into your garage to holler where no one can hear you, or pound your rage into a pillow. Keeping a journal is an excellent technique. Or you might consider writing a letter to the person who wronged you, and then holding a ritual where you burn the letter. Regular deep-breathing meditation is recommended by health-care professionals such as Herbert Benson, M.D., at the Harvard Mind/Body Institute.

You might try the gestalt technique of visualizing your offender sitting in a chair while you talk, scream, or cry your pain to the mental image. This lets you emotionally confront someone who is otherwise unreachable — for instance, a parent who has died.

My friend Don Campbell gave me the best advice. With his quiet faith, he started each day by saying, "No one owes me anything; yet I owe all things to all people." He assured me, if I'd repeat that affirmation, I'd free my life from petty resentments. "I'll sound like a wimp," I argued, but I agreed to try it. When the supermarket checkout clerk acted grouchy, I smiled at her anyway. When a friend missed an appointment, I released my irritation before calling her. And I discovered Don was right; it's like choosing forgiveness in advance. I was surprised at how free and peaceful I felt.

Always remember that forgiveness takes place within you, not between you and someone else.

In college, a sorority sister of my daughter, Sony, felt left out of a group of girls and wrote a letter that hurt Sony. In the years after college, whenever Sony saw her, she felt uncomfortable, remembering the letter. "I decided I had to forgive her," Sony told me. "So I thought about how hurt *she* must have felt to write her letter and how mature we'd both become, and I just let it go. I didn't have to say anything to her."

A lot of people get *stuck*; all they can remember is the pain of childhood, the hurt in their marriage, the unfairness on the job. Of course, you'll be unhappy if you hold on to bad memories! It's healthy to consciously deal with painful episodes from the past; but once we deal with them, *let them go*.

Forgiveness, after all, is not about fairness or justice; it's about inner peace, and the desire to feel happier. I talked to a woman in Erie, Pennsylvania, whose sixteen-year-old daughter was raped and murdered by the girl's high-school English teacher. For a dozen years, Betty clung to her hatred of the man, and who could blame her?

Paradoxically, though, the only way out of terrible suffering is through the gate of forgiveness. As long as we continue to hate, we give control of our mental, physical, and spiritual health to the person we hate. Bud Cooper, a Kansas City counselor, told me, "When you don't forgive, you give the other person a room in your mind, rent-free."

Everyone operates on his or her own timetable, though. My friend Laurie was brutally raped and nearly murdered several years ago. I asked her if she'd forgiven the rapist. "They never caught him," she said slowly, "so I never considered forgiving him. I'm still not sure I could, though the question has come up several times this past year, so I've started thinking about it."

Perhaps she will, perhaps she won't; forgiveness comes when a person is ready. If you want to forgive but find you can't, try forgiving for just one minute; then increase it to two, then three, and so on. When your first minute is up, if you need to return to anger, go ahead, and forgive yourself for doing so. But a little later, try forgiveness again, for one more minute.

After the drunk driver was convicted for killing her son, Nancy Hall sued him in civil court. When she won, she required him to write a two-hundred-dollar check once a month to MADD (Mothers Against Drunk Driving) and, on the check, to write, "In memory of Mark." Since prison regulations wouldn't let a prisoner write a check, his lawyer filled out the check, and the businessman wrote a monthly letter to Nancy from prison.

"In his letters, he told me how terrible he felt, until finally, I wrote back, and we began to correspond. Still, forgiveness snuck up on me. . . . I suppose it began when I started to see him as a human being." She pauses. "He's out of prison now and we appear together on stage, to give talks for MADD."

That's what is so amazing about forgiveness. It can take you places you never dreamed you could go, like on stage with the man who killed your son.

It's never easy. When Jesus called on us to forgive "seventy times seven," He meant, "Always." We are always called on to forgive. It comes to us through grace, for truly, who can do it alone? So we must pray for grace. And when it comes, it's "a miracle," as Dag Hammarskjöld wrote, "by which what is broken is made whole and what is soiled is again made clean."

Learning How to Love

Unable are the Loved to die
For Love is Immortality.

Emily Dickinson

Ever experienced this? You sit beside that special person in your life, feeling oh, so warm and loving . . . yet fifteen minutes later, the two of you are arguing.

Or you go through the grocery store checkout line without really seeing the cashier's face. He's just part of the machinery that totes up your food bill.

Ever averted your eyes as you pass a homeless person on a city street? Or put off calling a friend because you don't know what to say since her husband died?

Me, too.

Sometimes, the person I'm least loving to is — *me*.

Amazing, isn't it?

We carefully read cookbooks before baking a cake. Our computer manuals stay handy at our desks. And do you know anyone who skydives without a lesson or two?

Yet most of us leap into marriage or childbirth with no instruction at all. We fall in love or have babies and take, on faith, that we'll know how to do it right.

It's taken me half a lifetime to learn how little I know about love. I remember when a jewelry store in our city gave away pins for a holiday promotion. They read, "You are loved." People snatched them up.

But the real point is, not how to be loved; it's how *to* love. That's what the following stories are about.

6
God, My Mother, and Me

God looked a lot like my mother.

I never *consciously* thought that; but many years later, it made sense when I read, "Since, to small children, their parents are gods, our first perception of God reflects the way we regard our parents."

I grew up knowing that I could count on God (and my mother) but also knowing I'd better show God (and my mother) good behavior. I knew that God (and my mother) expected me to be a certain kind of person and I worked hard to live up to their expectations — to be the *good girl* that God (and my mother) wanted me to be.

It was an era of *earned grace*. I learned to count up my sins ("I talked back *once* to my mother, told *two* lies, and had *three* fights with my little brother") and do penance. I also experienced the awesome mystery of a Church ritual that gave even a young child the sense of generational continuum, of belonging to something extraordinary and long-lasting (which offered a bulwark of security in a dark and lonely universe).

I had no doubts, no existential questions in such a Church. As long as I worked hard to live up to the expectations of my mother and my Church, I fully expected to experience God's continuing favor. That meant living a happy life, life as it should be — a life that reflected the values I'd grown up with.

My mother expressed those values in a hundred different ways over the years. Not all were directly religious. I also heard, "Always wear clean underwear." "Never sit on public toilet seats." "Study hard and go to college." "Nice girls don't, not before marriage." "Marry well." "Raise good kids." "Keep your sterling silver polished." It all seemed part of being the good girl that my mother (and God) wanted me to be.

My life flowed easily in the direction I'd expected. Until, suddenly, terribly, God changed the rules.

Years later, I spoke before a large group of women, "I struck a bargain with God," I said. "As long as I was a good girl, God would be good to me, which meant I would live happily ever after. Anyone else strike a similar bargain?"

Hands went up. The crowd's laugh was rueful.

God failed me halfway through my twenty-ninth year when my first husband, John, died. Friends held my hands. "We're so sorry, Barbara." My mother, hushing her three small grandchildren, ordered food to serve after the funeral. My parish priest stumbled over hollow words meant to comfort, that didn't, while a voice inside me cried, *But how can this happen to a good girl who followed all the rules?*

The God I knew died along with John. I moved, empty-souled, through days in which the old rules no longer applied. I sat, for a time, in church pews, listening to words that had lost their meaning, until I refused to sit there again.

Without the comfort of church, I searched to fill the void. I found the women's movement. Gestalt therapy. Personal growth. A graduate degree. A career.

"I don't know you any more," cried my mother. "You've changed."

I looked at her over a chasm that widened. And widened. My values shifted, became my own. She felt repudiated. Her words grew angry, faded into consternation, hardened into querulous demands for me to be what I no longer had the power to be: her good Catholic daughter.

The years passed.

In 1984, my father died. Two years later, my mother learned she had cancer. "I'm sorry," said her doctor. "I give her three months. At most."

How small she looked — how frail — in her hospital bed. How was it, she loomed so large in my mind? I held her hand. My body filled, like a sponge, with unshed tears.

Our days together became islands of time, set apart from the rest of the world. I counted moments. Good moments when she wasn't in pain. Awful moments when her eyes grew dark with terror. Moments when we shared our memories and found, nestled in them, laughter. Our chasm of recent years was not so much crossed as simply . . . dissolved. We accepted each other.

The hospital chaplain dropped by daily. I could see, in the way my mother's shoulders relaxed, how it helped when he blessed her. I recalled the comfort of the Church. Did its structure help, in this, my mother's hardest journey?

Toward the end, I began to stay the night, dozing fitfully in my reclining chair, aware, always, of her breathing and the hospital noises — the clink of metal trays, the scuff of rubber-soled shoes, a beeper going off down the hall.

One morning, I came awake, instantly alert. The overused air held a sudden clarity. I realized — had I known it all along? — that God hadn't failed me when my young husband died. It was my view of God that had failed. God doesn't bargain. God *loves*. Grace isn't earned. Grace *is*.

I went to my mother's bed. Her breathing had changed. Instead of painful gasps, it had lightened, become soft. I touched her unconscious face. How white she seemed and how cold she felt. But on her hospital gown was pinned a pink ribbon rose. The floor nurse — a dark-skinned woman from India — had made it for her the night before. She'd held my hand and my mother's and prayed as if in gentle conversation.

I no longer saw God in the face of my mother. I saw, simply, my mother. A human being, who was not so large as I had imagined nor so strong nor so powerful nor so wise. A woman of virtue, a woman of faults. In a flash of insight, I understood — far more quickly than these words can tell it —

what it is that all parents must bear: the cross of their children perceiving them as gods.

In struggling to meet my mother's expectations (and God's) I had sometimes felt guilty or angry. But I'd placed expectations on God (and on my mother, too). Unreal expectations.

I'd missed the crucial point, that God's love comes *without* expectation. I am loved as I am. I am called to love God as God is. Not as I would have God be. And certainly not as a bargaining Deity who, if properly placated, can spare me the pain that is part of living — and growing.

A shaft of sunlight filtered through the Levelor blinds and rested on the pink ribbon rose. Gently, I touched the rose — then my mother's cold face. In seeing my mother as her real self, I let her go, and let go, at last, of my childish view of God.

It was as if T. S. Eliot had spoken in my ear: "I arrived where I had started . . . and knew the place for the first time."

7
Golden Scrapbooks of the Mind

On the day before his college graduation, my son Andy and I went strolling along an ocean beach. Suddenly, high above, two Navy fighter jets streaked past. I glanced at my tall, broad-shouldered son.

"Your father would be very proud of you," I said. An odd expression crossed Andy's face. "I've thought about Daddy a lot this year," he said with a catch in his voice. "You know what hurts? *I can't remember him.*"

Despite his linebacker's build, I suddenly glimpsed the shy, solemn four-year-old he had been when John's fighter jet crashed during the Vietnam war. "I've tried and tried, but I can't quite . . . touch him. I'm jealous of Sony, Mom, because she was older when he died. She has memories."

I was startled by a loss I had never thought about. My own memories spilled into my mind. John in his Navy dress-whites on our wedding day . . . my pride as I pinned on his wings when he graduated from flight school . . . his face, full of emotion, as he held his newborn daughter, and later, his sons.

I saw John — with Andy perched on his shoulder — exuberantly singing the song "Up, Up, and Away" into a blue California sky. As he sang, a hot-air balloon, in glowing colors, drifted by. How Andy had giggled in the joy of that moment! Afterward, whenever I heard that song, I saw that scene. But Andy couldn't remember it. No matter how hard he searched, his daddy could never be more than a figure glimpsed in the reflection of someone else's remembrance.

I thought about my mother's death. It seemed as if, everywhere I went, something awoke painful memories — the fragrance of her favorite perfume; a certain shade of blue; a

53

bubbly chuckle. And yet, how lucky I was to have those memories! Painful now, just as those of John had been after his death. But one day, I knew, the hurt would leave, and I would have a golden scrapbook in my mind. Through memories, I could forever reclaim my mother and my husband.

How often do we let the stuff of memories slip through our fingers? There are ways to fill our mental scrapbooks, of making and holding memories so we can keep those we love with us forever.

One way is *to make the ordinary memorable.* "Do something once and a child will turn it into a family tradition," said my friend Ben who has six children. Family ceremonies provide some of our most cherished memories.

I think how my children recall our camping tradition of Barbara Helen stories. And the later tradition of cutting our own Christmas tree.

To make the ordinary unforgettable requires only that we look at everyday events with eyes open to the symbolism they hold as a metaphor for love. Whether it's lighting the first fire of winter or enjoying the first summer picnic, it becomes memorable when we do it with appreciation and ceremony.

It's also important *to lock in special moments.* My friend Mary experienced two deaths before she turned eleven: her baby brother, then her father. Having learned how fragile life can be, she began, as a child, to make an effort to capture the lovely moments in her life.

"Whenever I sense that a moment is perfect," she told me, "I mentally file all the sensual details." Mary still vividly recalls a summer day when she was sixteen . . . the tingle of water drying on her skin as she sat by a lake . . . the pungent smell of steaks and lobsters on the grill . . . the wind brushing her shoulders and ruffling the lake water. Best of all, she remembers a happy awareness: *This day holds everything I've ever wanted.*

It's especially important to help children lock in special memories, because they seldom have long-term recall of early experiences. Now that she's grown, my daughter, Sony, makes a practice of sitting down several times a week with her son, Jake, to look through the family photo album. As Jake points to pictures of Grammy and Grandpa (Bill, my second husband), his mom talks about specific things Jake has done with us. Her reminders help cement the memories in his mind.

Try *to collect reminders.* My friend Vicki treasures a white snowball bush that grew from a cutting her grandmother carried westward eighty years ago. For Vicki, flowers are like snapshots, and her husband, Tom, gives her plants and bulbs on special occasions. "When I look at my garden, I don't see flowers," she said, "I see my Mother's Day mums or my Valentine's tulips. Each represents a special way Tom showed he loved me."

My own special reminder is an antique grandfather clock Mom bequeathed to me. Every hour when I hear its chimes — a rich double note — I feel, for an instant, a comforting sense of union with my parents, as if I have heard their voices.

Think carefully before you throw away love letters or your children's first-grade drawings! They're precious reminders. Don't assume that, because you're not interested at twenty-five in keeping family treasures, you'll feel the same way later in life.

Invest in future memories. "We've decided to give an anniversary party," said my mother. I listened, amazed, as she outlined her plans over the telephone. Why such an elaborate party on their forty-sixth anniversary?

But something in Mom's voice told me that this party was important — so important I decided to surprise my parents and take the children to California. I'll never forget the look on my parents' faces when we walked into their living room. The utter impracticality of our visit (because Sony was working and John and Andy were in college, we could only stay twenty-four hours) said louder than any words, "We love you."

As it turned out, Daddy would never see another anniversary. He died five months later. How glad I was then that I had given us all the memory of a happy surprise visit.

Into everyone's life come such opportunities. Sometimes it's a simple thing — a parent's decision on a lovely morning to forgo chores in favor of a hike through the woods with the kids. Or an impulsive visit to an elderly neighbor. It's the composite of such moments — moments when you take time for another person — that become a memory collage. Bits of kindness stick to pieces of caring, and they're all pasted together to form beautiful memories.

We can all *remember when* . . . Oh, the laughter that spills over as families hear stories they're heard a hundred times before and recall the events that each one knows by heart. It is in shared moments like these that families draw especially close.

We even translate pain into humor through "remember when's."

You know the kind of experience, when one person says with a sigh, "I suppose we'll laugh about this twenty years from now." And the truth is, you will!

But we should also take the time to listen when an older family member says, "I remember when . . ." One evening at our house, then eighty-six-year-old Grandpa Bartocci began reminiscing about the summers he spent as a boy at his grandmother's country estate near Genoa, Italy. I sneaked away from the dinner table and brought back a tape recorder. While his grandchildren listened, spellbound, he described his father's decision to immigrate to America and his own decision to follow. Today we have on tape a priceless account of Bartocci family history that we otherwise might have lost.

We build the best memories of all when we say, *"I love you."*

I'll never forget that night Daddy called spontaneously, "just to say I love you."

It's harder for some people than for others, but however abruptly, haltingly, or softly you say them to a parent, friend, child, or spouse, the words "I love you" will create the most important and most lasting memory of all.

The Christmas after my conversation with Andy on the beach, I gave my grown children an audiotape. We put it in the cassette player, and into our living room came the warm, laughing voice of a young man strumming a guitar. It was John Bartocci, Navy pilot, relaxing in his room aboard an aircraft carrier in 1968. "I'm going to sing some songs especially for you kids," came his voice, clear and alive. "Because your daddy misses you very much."

Their eyes glistened. Those vibrant words, saved on a tape that had nestled forgotten in a drawer all these years, gave Andy a chance to touch his dad at last. For finally he heard his father say directly to him, "I love you, son."

8
The Sixteenth Life of Old Tom

We are told that St. Francis said, "Make me a channel of
your peace. Where there is hatred, let me sow love." We are
called upon by God to love, but sometimes our teachers are
surprising — like the scrappy old tomcat I met just once but
remembered always.

It was a sun-washed Tuesday in early September when
my friend Terre responded to Mrs. Winters' phone call. Terre is
a blonde, pretty nurse who loves animals; she founded PAWS
(Pets Are Worth Safeguarding), an organization that arranges
for the neutering or humane death of pets belonging to the
elderly or handicapped.

Mrs. Winters was a shabby little lady of seventy-odd
years, badly crippled with arthritis. Her voice was halting and
apologetic. "It's about this cat . . ." and she led Terre outside to
meet Tom — the biggest, oldest, ugliest, sickest alley cat Terre
had ever seen.

He lay on a splintered board on the paint-blistered porch
behind Mrs. Winters' run-down apartment house, one paw
stretched out in pain. His ears were scabbed black from ear
mites. Two deep, blood-encrusted cuts ran down his yellow
tabby-striped back. His face was oddly distorted, the mouth
pulled askew as if with a harelip, although whether the defect
was congenital or the result of some fight, Terre couldn't tell.
Even though his body was emaciated, he looked as big as two
ordinary cats.

"Old Tom's been coming around for sixteen years," said
Mrs. Winters. "Never lets you pet him or nothing. But me and
the neighbors, we leave him food. Kind of cheered us up, to see

old Tom." She paused, as if distracted. "He's been gone awhile though, and now he's so sick . . ." her birdlike voice trembled. "I sure didn't want to see him die, but I don't have money for a doctor."

Mrs. Winters, thought Terre, *this cat will be dead by morning.* But aloud, she replied, "Sixteen years? That's pretty old for a cat. Are you sure it's always been Tom?"

The old lady nodded. "Oh, yes. Mrs. Giraldi — she lived upstairs until her stroke last year — she said Tom's gone through all nine lives and then some."

I believe it, thought Terre, *but he's run out of lives now.*

Mrs. Winters put a gnarled hand on Terre's arm and confided, "Old age and hard times never licked Tom before. No, sir, never did."

As if he felt their attention, the cat suddenly lifted his head. He seemed to stare directly at Terre. His eyes, like the rest of him, were yellow, and hard and shiny, like marbles. True cat's eyes. He had a tough, unflinching stare, and reminded Terre of one of her patients, an irascible old man on kidney dialysis. The old man would mutter at the machine, "I'm going to beat you yet, you devil. Wait and see."

She patted Mrs. Winters' hand. "Sixteen years is a long life for a cat. And he looks pretty sick."

"But sick don't mean dead," she replied with sudden and unexpected grit in her voice. "Not if he gets the right help."

"I'll take him to a vet I know," said Terre. *At least I can have him humanely put to sleep,* she thought.

While Mrs. Winters hovered, making little bird noises, Terre gingerly picked up the cat. She knew he was too sick to fight her. His eyes blinked once when, despite her care, she jarred his injured paw. Otherwise, he was quiet as she carried him to her car and deposited him on the right front seat.

"You know he might not make it," she warned Mrs. Winters. The crippled old lady nodded. Tears winked at the corners of her eyes. "But you got to keep trying. Hear me, old Tom? You got to try."

On the seat beside Terre, Tom pulled himself into a sitting position. His yellow eyes stared at her. She felt a peculiar sensation, as if his eyes were saying, "Well, I've been around sixteen years and no one has loved me yet. Now some stranger is taking me off to die. Why should I be surprised?"

"That's not fair," she said aloud. "I didn't get you into this."

But when Dr. Abbot said, "Looks like a candidate for kitty heaven," she blurted, to her own surprise, "No. Try to save him."

"Save this old alley cat?" the vet asked — no, exclaimed — with an incredulous look on his face.

"Please. Do everything you can."

Terre returned to the animal clinic a week later. Tom was sitting up, his paw no longer held out in pain. Under medication, the cuts on his back had started to heal. Only his ears were still in bad shape, black and nearly deformed from years of infestation from ear mites.

"How are you?" inquired Terre. Tom responded by backing away. The harelip contorted his face. Yet his yellow eyes seemed to watch her even closer than before.

"I can treat him at home for his ears," she said.

The vet shrugged. "Okay. But this cat's been nearly wild for years. I don't think you'll make a pet of him."

"Who said I wanted to?" she responded.

Terre's hospital schedule kept her away all day and she didn't want Tom to run loose in the yard, so she borrowed a large dog crate and set it up in her basement. For a month, he lived there while she trained him to use a sandbox. Each day, she treated his ears for the painful, itching ear mites. Her other cat, Twerp, stayed upstairs. Tom had enough to handle, figured Terre; he didn't need to cope with another cat. Not yet.

In the evenings, when she opened the crate, he would back into a corner until Terre moved a safe distance away. Then, gingerly, he would poke his yellow head around the door. A twitching. A sniffling. Slowly one paw, then another, would emerge, until at last, with a certain weathered dignity, he would stand beside the kennel. *Like an old soldier at parade rest,* she thought.

After she told Mrs. Winters where Tom was, the old lady called every day, her thin birdlike voice fluttering through the receiver, "Is he still getting better?"

"He gets better every day," said Terre. Tom's body had started to fill out. Only his ears continued to be a major problem. They itched terribly and he rubbed against anything he could find, which only tore the scabs open again.

Still, Terre thought Tom was in good enough shape to visit Mrs. Winters.

When the bent old lady opened her door, her eyes grew almost young in their gladness. "Will you look at Tom! It's a miracle!"

"He's still not completely well," cautioned Terre.

The shabby old lady and the veteran alley cat eyed each other. "Don't you worry none," said Mrs. Winters, a note of new confidence in her voice. "Old Tom's going to make it. Why, it makes sense to stay alive when someone cares, don't it?"

Terre put her arm around the old woman's frail shoulders. "Yes, it does," she said gently.

Several days later, Terre moved Tom upstairs. He'd been with her for six weeks now and no longer retreated when she approached, but he never let her pet him.

She wasn't sure how Tom and Twerp would get along. They eyed each other warily when she introduced them. Twerp was a mixture of Burmese and Persian with long, whitish-brown fur.

He and Tom circled each other while Terre held her breath; then, Tom sat down. His body language seemed to say, "I'm out of the picture. Do whatever you please." In a few minutes, Twerp sauntered off, finding his own favorite spot on the sofa. After that, they mostly ignored each other, like elderly roommates who share a house but haven't much else in common.

Thanksgiving approached. The week before, an envelope arrived, full of wrinkled bills. Terre pulled out the accompanying letter. "I been saving my money," read the crabbed handwriting. "I don't have much but I wanted to give something to PAWS so you can save other old cats. It's not the end just because you're old."

Terre blinked. The envelope held nearly fifty dollars from Mrs. Winters, a woman who had barely enough to live on. "Well, old warrior," she said to Tom, "what should I do about this?"

Because Tom was so averse to being held, she used her voice as a caress. Tom seemed to like it. When she talked to him, he sat about three feet away, his yellow eyes on her face, his head tilted, as if listening.

"We'll hurt her feelings if we return the money," said Terre. "But how can we properly thank her?"

An idea struck her. At different times, they'd had a mascot for PAWS. Why not Tom? Who better than this ancient warrior who had survived a lifetime of indignities?

She wrote a letter. "Dear Mrs. Winters: Thank you for giving money to save old cats and for bringing me help when I needed it. I've been offered a job with PAWS to become their mascot. What do you think? (signed) Tom Cat. P.S. Terre invites you to Thanksgiving dinner."

Three days later, Terre's phone rang. "You really want to make Tom your mascot?" Mrs. Winters' birdlike voice trilled with excitement.

"Yes, we do."

The older woman cleared her throat. "It just goes to show, don't it? Being old don't mean you're worn out. Don't mean there's no place for you."

"No, it doesn't," said Terre gently.

On Thanksgiving, Mrs. Winters wore a pink silk dress that smelled faintly of camphor, and she offered with shy pride a bowl of homemade cranberry relish.

I was invited for dinner, too. That's how I learned about old Tom. "So you're the lady who rescued him," I said to Mrs. Winters. "He's a lucky cat."

She smiled. "He don't quit, does he?"

"Neither do you." We sat down to dinner while Tom eyed us from a corner.

"He doesn't like to be touched or held," explained Terre. "So I talk to him instead."

I left soon after dinner, and Terre drove Mrs. Winters home. When she got back to her place, she cleaned up the kitchen, then settled on the living-room sofa. Tom sat three feet away, watching.

"I love you, Tom," said Terre. His head tilted. His yellow eyes examined her face. "It's true. I tell my patients how you won't quit, and they shouldn't either."

Tom blinked. Suddenly, Terre felt a peculiar weight in her lap. And heard a strange, rumbling noise.

Tom had jumped to her lap and was purring! For a moment, she was too stunned to move. She placed her hand on his back. He didn't flinch, just looked at her with his tough yellow eyes. As surely as if he spoke, he seemed to say: "I'm home now." Perhaps, thought Terre, it's the closest old Tom has ever come to love.

9
A Gift From the Heart

Who could forget such a birthday? "Barbara," Bill announced, "your gift is in the freezer." Our teenage kids giggled and pranced around, barely able to contain themselves. Mystified, I went to the freezer — and broke out laughing. There, inside, festively wrapped, was a round, three-gallon ice-cream container. My "addiction" to ice cream is legendary in our household.

But a few minutes later, as I pulled off the wrappings, I laughed even harder. Bill loves surprising me — and he had done it again! There was no ice cream in the container. Instead, there were four large handcrafted wooden numbers for the front of our house. Bill had heard me say, a few months earlier, how I'd always wanted big easy-to-read house numbers. I was touched and delighted. And I loved the fun of his "double surprise."

My gift also had special meaning because only a week before, I'd bumped into a good friend at one of our downtown department stores. Marjorie was returning an anniversary gift that her husband had given her. "Wouldn't you think, after twenty years, that George would know I never wear gold?" She said it jokingly, but I could hear the slight hurt.

As I stood with my family a week later, laughing over my new house numbers, I compared these two styles of gift-giving. George had probably spent several hundred dollars on jewelry his wife didn't really care for. Bill had spent thirty dollars for a gift that was *just right*: something for me alone, something he had planned and thought about.

Sometimes the right gift isn't something you wrap up. When my stepson, Marc, graduated from college, his father took him on a fishing trip into the Canadian wilderness. Such a week may never come again, now that Marc has married and has a family. But those seven days created a special bonding where two men became more than father and son — they became adult *friends*.

To give the right gift takes time and effort, and a willingness to know someone. Rosita Perez whooped with delight as she told me about her favorite gift. She walked into her living room on her eighteenth wedding anniversary and stared, incredulous, at a five-foot-high wooden dollhouse. It was the dollhouse she'd yearned for as a child — but never received. Her husband, Ray, said softly, "Happy anniversary, Rosie." Ever since that day Rosita has spent hours painting, wallpapering, and furnishing the dream-come-true gift. "My husband's a tough cop," she told me, "but he gave me the most sensitive gift I've ever received."

Just as sensitive, in a different way, was the gift Bonnie gave Tod. I've known Tod for seventeen years. When he opened his forty-fifth-birthday gift from his wife, Bonnie, tears sprang to his eyes. Inside a small box was a gift certificate for a ski trip. "You mean it?" he asked with a lump in his throat. She nodded. You see, the real gift was more than the trip. Years earlier, Bonnie had persuaded Tod to give up skiing because, she said, "it's too expensive now that we have children." Yet, for Tod, skiing down a wintry mountain slope brought real inner renewal. His gnawing unhappiness over the promise she'd extracted created a fissure in their marriage. Bonnie's gift, after several months of marriage counseling, symbolized her acceptance of her husband's need, even though she didn't understand it.

When you give a gift you don't understand, or maybe, think is a little weird — like something for your teenage son! — you're really giving the message *You're okay. I love you as you are.* For my sister-in-law Mary Shirley, the message came in the shape of a butterfly, fashioned into a golden pin, from the special man in her life. "To me, the butterfly symbolizes the soul," Mary explained. "Ian didn't share my spiritual beliefs, but his gift showed — beautifully — that he accepted them in me."

Acceptance is never more special than when it occurs between a parent and child. Just ask my banker-friend, Bill Burkhart. In 1952, he played football for the University of Missouri. Twenty years later, when his son Mark entered Mizzou's rival, Kansas State University, there was a lot of good-natured family joshing. Imagine Bill's surprise when Mark, in the midst of a busy sophomore year, took time to *needlepoint* a roaring Mizzou tiger for his father's Christmas gift. Mark's gift showed that he saw his father as a person, as well as a parent, and acknowledged his own change in status to young adult.

There's another kind of acceptance — the kind Dr. Hank Cankowski brought to my dear friend Lois Gubitosi. When Hank heard Lois had exploratory surgery scheduled, he knew the terrifying question was: Would she emerge cancer-free? So Hank took his friend a papier-mâché puppet he'd purchased in Mexico: a clown that smilingly dangled from a parachute. Hooking it to Lois's IV stand, he said gently, "This is your '*let go and let God*' puppet." As Lois waited for the lab reports, her eyes strayed continually to the smiling puppet. "I was overjoyed when the nodes turned out to be negative," she told me later, "but by then, I was at peace either way. I had let go." Hank's puppet was the catalyst.

It takes observation to fill a need that hasn't been recognized yet. When Sharon Kelly unpacked in her college dorm, she found something unexpected in her suitcase. During her daughter's high-school senior year, Frances Staley reread the New Testament and made marginal notes of passages that held special meaning for her. Then she tucked the Bible in Sharon's suitcase. Whenever her new college life seemed scary, Sharon opened her Bible. It was like talking to her mother.

To gift someone, try listening. So often we're focused on our own worries that we listen with only half an ear.

My mom knew how to listen. She kept a small notebook in her kitchen drawer, and jotted down gift ideas as she heard them. Every Christmas morning, someone would cry, "Mom! How did you *know* I wanted this?" Mom merely smiled. No one even knew about her notebook; we discovered it after she died.

Isn't the greatest gift of all really the gift of *time*? A longtime friend, Bobbi Ellison, spent seven long months in a hospital bed, recovering from spinal surgery. Her husband, Joe — a senior Navy captain with a demanding job in the Office of the Assistant Secretary of Defense — often had to work fourteen- to sixteen-hour days during those months. Yet every single day, Joe found time to visit Bobbi in the hospital. He'd take some little gift — flowers or a bracelet or a miniature alarm clock; but the real gift, for Bobbi, came in the *dailiness* of his visits. Giving her his time when he had such a hectic working schedule vividly showed how much he really cared.

Giving time or talent often returns something unexpected. My parents decided to host a large party to celebrate their forty-sixth wedding anniversary. It was a sudden decision that seemed so important to my mother that I flew the three kids and myself to California as a surprise. We had to return right after the party because of the kids' work and school schedules, which made the plane fare *very* expensive; but, somehow, I felt it *mattered* that we go.

Well, my father died before their next anniversary, and our spontaneous trip was the last time his grandchildren saw him alive. Our gift to my parents turned out to be a gift to us.

Sometimes, *only* the gift of time will say what you really mean. My friend Diane Vogel received an extraordinary gift from her stepdaughter, Jonne. Jonne was fourteen when Diane married her father, and they'd had some rough times. Yet, gradually, a closeness developed, and when Jonne turned twenty-one, she invited Diane to a private "adoption ceremony" in which Jonne "adopted" her as her true *other mother*.

The right gift doesn't need a special occasion. My son John will surprise his wife at work with delivery of a single rose in a bud vase — always a spontaneous "I love you" gesture. Giving a gift *just because* . . . well, it says, more clearly than any words, *you* matter to me.

And how about saying "Thank you" with a gift tied to an unexpected holiday? Rosemarie Kitchin, a longtime friend in Philadelphia, travels a lot in her job and depends on an airport van service. Instead of a traditional Christmas gift, she marched into the van office one Halloween with a bushel basket of apples and a note that read, "You never trick me; you always treat me. Thanks a lot for great service! Rosemarie."

The key to spontaneous gift-giving is taking enough time to *really think* about a special person. It means noticing potential gifts as we follow our daily routines: a jar of pickled herring or macadamia nuts at the supermarket for your spouse; a mug you see that's imprinted with your friend's name; a new cassette by your aunt's favorite singer. I once worked with a man who kept on hand a book of ice-cream coupons. When one of Walt's co-workers had a rough day, or did a good job, a coupon for a free double-dip appeared mysteriously on the worker's desk. "It's better than chicken soup," Walt explained with a twinkle in his eye.

I gave a memorable gift one summer when Bill and I vacationed in Colorado. Bill had wandered into a western shop where he saw a belt buckle embossed with a sterling-silver eagle. Eagles are significant to Bill. He loved the buckle, but the price tag convinced him it was too expensive, so he put it back. Thirty minutes later, I wandered into the same shop, saw the same belt buckle, knew Bill would love it, and bought it. What mattered to him, more than the buckle itself, was realizing I had *known* how much it would mean to him, and that I bought it out of love for him.

The right message delivered at the right time can also be an extraordinary gift.

Ron Meiss, who travels the world as a professional speaker, chuckled as he told me about the high-school graduation gift he got from his father. "A Dale Carnegie course! Can you imagine how *under*-whelmed a seventeen-year-old boy was with that? I wanted a car!" Yet Ron's father saw something special in his son; and that course, Ron is now convinced, brought out in him the skills and confidence he needed to embark on his successful speaking career.

Something similar happened to my friend Janet Reimer. She was a full-time wife and mother when she began to paint seriously. Soon she was invited to hang her work in a local art show. "I was so excited when one sold," relates Janet, "but puzzled, too, because I couldn't find out who the buyer was. Two months later, I dropped in at my husband's office, and there, above Ron's desk, was my painting. He'd bought it anonymously to encourage me!" Though Janet now sells her paintings regularly, she's never forgotten the gift of her husband's quiet faith when she first started.

Inside every one of us exists a desire to leave some kind of legacy. Whenever we help someone reach his or her potential, we'll feel as if we contributed to that legacy. Barbara Loots, a friend who writes for Hallmark Cards, remembers her senior year in college, when one of her favorite instructors was named a distinguished professor — which brought a five-hundred-dollar honorarium. The next day, five hundred dollars mysteriously appeared in the bank account of a needy student friend, allowing her to enroll in graduate school. "Our prof never did own up that he was the secret gift giver, but *we knew*. His gift to her encouraged all of us."

The greatest gift giver is God. Through Jesus Christ, He gave us salvation. Unearned, freely given, coming to us wrapped in love. All we have to do is accept our gift. I wonder why we make it so hard?

10
The Waiting Parent

A few years ago, I went to Wisconsin to give a workshop to ministers. My topic was not exactly ministerial. I'd been asked to talk about writing.

A group of fifty met at a lakeside resort an hour outside of Chicago. The June sun felt warm, the ministers were friendly, and the lake waters looked inviting; but my mind kept jumping from the workshop to a family problem. My stepdaughter Linda had angrily told her father the week before: "I never want to see you again!" She resented his questions about some decisions she was making. At nineteen, she lived on her own, and we couldn't order her to be part of our family. But I saw how wounded the encounter left Bill, and I felt sad and helpless. How could we change Linda's mind?

As my workshop ended, the large group broke into twos and threes, and people began strolling around the lush green lawn. A minister from Illinois, Richard Thomas, wandered in my direction. We'd met at breakfast, and I liked him. The Reverend Thomas was a tall, slightly stoop-shouldered man with blue eyes that crinkled at the corners. Yet I saw in the depths of those eyes something deeper, like pain.

Now we chatted for a few minutes, the casual conversation of acquaintances.

Then he said, "You seem bothered by something."

I sighed. Perhaps it was the kindness in his eyes, coupled with that edge of something more; suddenly, I blurted out my worries about Linda. "If only she understood how much Bill loves her," I ended.

"You do have a problem," agreed the minister. We had walked toward a couple of chairs near the lake, and it seemed natural to sit down.

"I understand what you're experiencing," he continued. "Three weeks ago, I stood in a telephone booth on the campus of my daughter's college. I could look through the glass and see the very building where she lives, but Lisa's voice was like ice. 'I'm sorry, Dad,' she said. 'I don't want to see you.'"

I must have looked surprised, because he smiled ruefully. "No one's immune from family problems, not even ministers, although I once thought we were." Then he went on:

The night I called Lisa, I held the telephone, long after the dial tone sounded. The evening was warm, I remember, but I felt cold. I'd come to Lisa's college to give a speech, but what I really wanted was to see her.

I walked to my car. Cicadas sang in the bushes, and a car's headlights flashed. The air seemed thick and humid.

I wondered again: *How could I, a minister, someone whose whole life is devoted to helping others, be so estranged from my own child?* The question had haunted me for months. I'd lie in bed at night, eyes wide open, staring at nothing. I'd get up in the morning and feel the question thudding in my chest like a dull ache. It was with me when I counseled other parents.

I never thought our family would face the kinds of problems that I counseled other people about. Phyliss and I waited ten years to have a child, while I went through seminary. When we learned she was pregnant, we were ecstatic. Lisa was a joy to raise. Tiny, like her mother, with the same blonde coloring, and with the most wonderful laugh — like Tinkerbell in *Peter Pan*. From the time she was small, we'd hear people say, "What a darling child. You must be so proud of her!" We *were* proud.

We live in a nice Chicago suburb, the kind with tree-shaded streets and split-level homes. You know, where you see joggers on the streets and kids riding bikes. It's a good place to raise a family.

A lot of my ministry involved counseling, and I was a good counselor. Yet other people's problems always seemed just a little bit — well, removed. Everything flowed so smoothly for our family. You can see it in our photo albums: snapshots of Lisa, shyly smiling at her first piano recital . . . leaving for Girl Scout Camp . . . looking pretty in her first prom dress . . .

We weren't surprised when she graduated with honors and gave the commencement address at her high-school graduation. She did everything well. In fact, she got more upset than we did when she was less than perfect.

"Did I sound okay?" she asked after her commencement speech. I could hear her anxiety, and I gave her a big hug. "You sounded great, sweetheart." She sighed with relief.

Lisa went off to college that fall. We saw her at Thanksgiving and Christmas, but it was summer before we noticed the change in her.

"I suppose we'll have kids all over the place," Phyliss had said, the week before Lisa arrived. "There goes our peace and quiet." But her eyes twinkled, and I laughed, too. Both of us could hardly wait to fill the house with Lisa's friends. We'd missed the noise and hullabaloo.

But Lisa seemed quiet, even withdrawn.

Usually, the three of us chattered at dinner, but now she seemed far away. She hardly spoke, and Phyliss said later, "Did you see what she ate? A bird would eat more!"

I grinned. "So? She's dieting. It's what you always tell me to do."

But a few nights later, I looked more closely at Lisa's plate. A single tomato slice, some lettuce, and three peas. *Three peas?* When I urged her to eat more, she shook her head and said, "I'm not hungry tonight, Daddy."

The dinner atmosphere, needless to say, was strained. *Could Lisa be depressed?* I wondered. Phyliss and I watched her afterward, as she walked down the hall to her bedroom. The light caught her — just so — and I saw, for a moment, her silhouetted profile. It startled me. Her arms and shoulders had a — a boniness to them. Lisa wasn't just slender, she was downright skinny.

She'd accepted a job at the library — where she'd worked the summer before — so we didn't see her during the day. My ministry keeps me busy all day long, anyway, and sometimes into the evenings. It was nearly a week before Phyliss cornered me.

"Something's wrong," she said with a slight tremor in her voice.

"About Lisa?"

"Yes. Her friends aren't coming around. The house is like a tomb. When Lisa's not working, she disappears into her room. I'm worried."

"A boyfriend?"

"I don't think so."

I had a commitment that evening, but the next day, I asked Lisa to go for a walk with me after work.

"I'm pretty tired, Daddy."

"Honey, this isn't like you. What's going on?"

She merely shrugged.

A few days later, as I worked on my Sunday sermon in my office, Phyliss called. "Hurry! Meet me at the hospital. Lisa's collapsed!"

I practically dropped the phone as I rushed out. We met in the Emergency Room. It seemed forever before the doctor emerged from examining her. "Reverend Thomas," he asked quietly, "are you familiar with *anorexia nervosa*?"

When he said the words, everything fell into place. Of course! I knew about the eating disorder, and that the most likely victims are between the ages of twelve and twenty-five — generally middle-class girls and young women who want to be "perfect."

But our daughter? I didn't want to believe it.

We signed Lisa into the hospital that day. But it wasn't our sweet, loving daughter who screamed at us from her bed, "I won't eat! You can't make me! Do you hear? You can't make me!"

Phyliss wept, and so did I.

The next few weeks seemed to last forever.

Lisa's doctor warned us, "Treating anorexia means more than making someone eat. The patient has to change her distorted perception of herself. Unfortunately, about twenty-five percent of anorexics are not helped by treatment. They remain vulnerable to a relapse."

Phyliss and I both talked to a therapist, but Lisa refused to.

"Did we push her too hard?" asked Phyliss. "We never meant to. I thought she liked to earn good grades. I thought she enjoyed all her activities."

"Lisa's created unreal expectations for herself," said Dr. Brunner, our therapist. "Parents do demand more from firstborn or only children, but some children expect too much of themselves. Any activity, no matter how small, has to be done perfectly, or they feel like failures. They get angry. Lisa's taking out her anger on her own body."

Finally, she did begin to eat a little, but food was like bad-tasting medicine, to be gulped down. In August, her doctor said she could return to college if she would meet regularly with a physician on campus. She agreed.

But some connecting link had broken between us. Lisa never wrote or called that fall. And at Christmas, she went to a friend's home, a girl who lived in another state.

"What did we do wrong?" asked Phyliss, weeping. "She seems to hate us. Yet we felt so close to her while she was growing up."

"Give her time," said Dr. Brunner.

But nothing had changed by spring when I showed up on campus to give my speech. Lisa didn't want to see me.

I walked back to my room where I was staying, as discouraged as I've ever been. All year, I'd prayed, but it seemed as if none of my prayers had been heard.

As we sat beside the lake in Wisconsin, the Reverend Thomas confided in me, "Sometimes people think ministers have an easier time of it, that we never doubt or lose faith. But I came close to despair that evening."

The sun had dropped on the horizon, making streaks of pink and red across the undulating water. I swatted a mosquito.

"What happened?"

"Something that may apply to your situation," he said, and smiled briefly. "I went to my room and sat down to pray, but no words came. I felt wrapped in a gray fog. My window was half open — I never use air-conditioning if I don't have to — and a light breeze made a tree branch rattle on my window. Out of habit, I reached for my Bible, but it slipped from my hand. When I picked it up off the floor, it was open to a passage in Luke, Luke 15:11. I could almost recite the words by heart: 'A man had two sons and the younger asked for his portion of goods and journeyed to a far country . . .' "

"The story of the prodigal son!" I exclaimed.

"That's what most of us call it. But that night, I read the words in a different light. Suddenly, I realized that it's also the story of 'The Waiting Parent.' The father in the story let his youngest son go, and though the son went off and squandered his inheritance, the father waited. When the son returned home — remember these words? — *he had compassion and ran and fell on his son's neck and kissed him. And he said, 'My son was lost and is found.'*

"The father let his son go. Yet he never gave up. He waited, in case his son should return. And I realized, that's what God does. He lets us go, yet He's always there, waiting with compassion for us to return. Our Waiting Father . . .

"That's when I knew I had to be Lisa's Waiting Father. Our counselor told us, 'She's a young adult. She has to make her own way.' But I didn't want to listen. I wanted to *make* Lisa come back to me. And I can't. So I love her and wait."

The lake water lapped the shore in a mesmerizing, even rhythm. "What if she doesn't come back?" I finally ventured.

In the twilight, the minister said softly, "You follow our Father's example. You keep on loving. And waiting."

The Power of Prayer

The more I pray, the fewer coincidences there are in my life.

Anonymous

Do you pray?

Maybe you pray in ways you don't realize.

When my two-year-old grandson Jake squeals with laughter and jumps up and down on his "happy feet," isn't he offering a joyful prayer?

When my husband, Bill, fixes my computer instead of watching the ball game, isn't he offering a prayer of love?

When the atheist, driving down the highway, sees a car coming at him — head-on — and cries in terror, "Oh-my-God!" isn't he offering a prayer?

And aren't those prayers heard?

Prayer is all about communication.

In words.

Body language.

Deeds.

It's how we talk to God.

And how God talks to us, and *through* us.

Have you ever encountered just the right message — one you needed to hear at a certain time in your life — and it came from a friend, or in a book, or even from someone on TV?

Have you ever experienced a mysterious coincidence? You're an engineer who wants to change jobs. Someone you meet for the first time says, "Our company is looking for an engineer. Know anyone?"

Those are prayers, listened to and heard.

When my grandson Jake celebrated his first birthday, we had a backyard picnic, and his proud daddy pulled out a video camera. Later, watching the tape, we were astonished to hear a raucous noise over little Jake's head, as he sat in his high chair eating cake.

Cheeep, cheeeep, cheeep, cheeeep.

It was a bird. The noisiest bird I'd ever heard.

What astonished us is this: At the picnic, we hadn't heard the bird. He'd been making a racket, but we'd tuned him out.

I think we do that to God.

God does answer our prayers . . . though not always as we expect. We have to be open.

Cheeep, cheeeeep, cheeeep.

11
The Hour That Changed My Life

It was my birthday that February morning, but I didn't feel birthday-ish. I felt harried as I grabbed my briefcase and headed for a business breakfast. Life had been good to me overall. My small advertising agency was thriving. Husband Bill and the kids were doing fine. Yet something seemed to be missing — something that didn't even have a name. I felt it only as a small emptiness inside.

At the restaurant I joined Don Campbell, a tall lantern-jawed man of some sixty years. He was a successful marketing consultant with an unusual empathy for people. I was always struck by his calm, peaceful manner.

Over poached eggs we discussed an advertising project and then, business behind us, I mentioned my birthday and confessed to my nagging feeling of emptiness.

"Want to fill it?" Don asked.

"Sure. But how?"

"Start your day with an hour of prayer."

"I don't have time for that!" I gasped.

"Exactly what I said twenty years ago. I was president of a Chicago ad agency and running every which way just to keep up. I believed in daily prayer but couldn't find time for it. I had the sinking feeling that my life was getting out of control. Then a friend told me I was going about things backward.

" 'You're trying to fit God into your life,' he said. 'Five minutes here, ten minutes there. You need to fit your life around God, and you do that with a commitment. An hour a day — now *that's* commitment.' The idea is to take a chunk of time big enough to mean something to you — and then, give that chunk to God."

Don's eyes twinkled as he continued, "I thought my friend was off his rocker. To find an extra hour for God, I'd have to get up an hour earlier. I'd lose sleep and ruin my health." The twinkle turned into a grin. "But I haven't been sick in twenty years."

Twenty years!

I left the restaurant in turmoil. An hour of prayer? Preposterous! Yet I couldn't get Don's idea out of my mind.

Saying nothing to our three teenagers or to Bill, I set my alarm for 5:00 A.M. We lived in the Midwest and oh, it's cold and dark at five in the morning in February. I wanted to curl back up under the blanket, but I forced myself to get up.

The house wrapped around me, dark and gloomy. I tiptoed to the living room, ignoring Burt, our Labrador retriever, and settled on the couch. It was peculiar being alone with God. No church rituals. Just me. And God. For an hour.

I glanced at my watch and cleared my throat. "Well, God, here I am. Now what?"

I would love to report that God replied immediately, but there was only quiet. As I watched the first tinges of sunrise I tried to pray, but thought instead of my son Andy and the fight we'd had the day before. I thought about a client whose business had hit a rough spot. I thought of inconsequential things.

Yet, gradually, my erratic thoughts slowed. My breathing slowed, too, until I sensed a stillness within me. I grew aware of small sounds — the refrigerator hum, Burt's tail slapping the floor, a frozen branch brushing a window. Then I felt the warm presence of love. I know of no other way to describe it. The air, the very place in which I sat, seemed to change, as the ambiance of a house will change when someone you love is home.

I had been sitting for fifty minutes, but only then did I really begin to pray. And I discovered I wasn't praying with my usual hurried words or my list of "gimmes."

All my life I'd been *told* God loves me. On that cold February morning, I *felt* God's love, and the immensity of it was so overwhelming that I sat in quiet thanksgiving for nearly fifteen minutes. Then Andy's alarm went off and Burt gave a small *Woof.* The ordinary day had begun. But all through the rest of that day, I felt warmed by the memory of that love.

The next morning the house seemed even darker and colder than before. But, shivering, I did get up. *One more day,* I thought.

And the next day, *One more day.*

Day by single day, a dozen years passed.

There have been plenty of crises in those years: difficulty with one of our teenagers, marital turbulence, a big financial loss. Through every crisis, I found a quietness of soul in that hour with God. I read the Bible and spiritual literature; I write in my prayer journal; and most of all, I sit in prayerful contemplation.

It gives me time to put things in perspective, to find God in every circumstance. Once I find God, there seems to be no problem that cannot be resolved.

Some mornings, I am quickly filled with the wonder and glory of God. But other mornings, I feel nothing. That's when I remember something else Don Campbell said: "There will be times when your mind just won't go into God's sanctuary. That's when you spend your hour in God's waiting room. Still, you're there, and God appreciates your struggle to stay there. What's important is your commitment."

Because of it, my life is better.

Starting my day with an hour of prayer filled my empty space to overflowing and changed my life.

12
The Unexpected Answer

It was an ordinary spring day. I was looking at greeting cards, hunting for a birthday card for my husband. Suddenly, I laughed aloud at one card. "Sweetheart," it read, "you're the answer to my prayers." And inside: "You're not what I prayed for exactly, but apparently you're the answer."

Only the night before, I had said in exasperation, "Honestly, Bill, you're sure not the husband I dreamed about."

He had grinned and hugged me. "But I'll bet our marriage is better than you ever imagined."

I took the card home. While I wrapped Bill's gift, I thought about all the times when it seemed as if my prayers had gone unanswered.

As a little girl, I prayed that my father would settle our family in Durango, Colorado, where my grandparents lived. He was in the Army and we moved so often! I yearned to put down roots.

Yet, how often, as a grownup, had I said, "I appreciate my childhood! I learned so much, living in all those places."

As a widow with three young children to raise, my hopes centered on a job as a writer in Washington, D.C. But the job offer didn't come. Instead, a Midwestern greeting-card company invited me to join its staff.

Not what I prayed for exactly, I thought, but if I hadn't moved here, I would never have met Bill. And what a difference he had made in my life and the children's.

At our birthday dinner that night, Bill laughed loudly when he read his card. He, too, remembered our earlier conversation. "Not bad," he said, grinning. "This card carries some pretty profound wisdom."

Not long after that, our daughter came home from high school, looking happy but puzzled. "Remember how awful I felt when I didn't get the part in the school play?"

Of course we remembered! Bill and I had ached for her.

A smile blossomed. "Well, I've been asked to go with the debating team to the out-of-state tournament. I've wanted to do that for three years. Isn't it strange? If I'd gotten the part in the play, I wouldn't be able to go."

Bill and I looked at each other. "Not what she prayed for exactly . . ." he began. "But apparently the answer!" we ended together.

Later that same year, Bill's young consulting business received an unusual offer. Bill was asked to take an eighteen-month assignment in a small town four hours away. For a struggling new business, it seemed like the answer to a prayer — except that Bill would have to live there.

What should we do? We drove to the town, a tiny community of four thousand people. Sony would be a senior in the fall. Bravely, she said, "It's okay. I can change schools."

But my job was challenging and rewarding. Could I afford to leave it? And what about the boys? Our son John was starting high school; Andy was a shy seventh grader.

Bill and I anguished over our decision. In tears one night, I went driving and wound up in a small church. Sitting in near-darkness, I prayed: *Bill needs this work, but is it worth the upheaval to move? What should we do?*

When I woke the next morning, I felt surprisingly peaceful. "I think you should take the job, Bill. But the children and I will stay here."

He looked at me carefully. "That's not what I prayed for exactly . . ."

For the first time in days, I smiled. "But apparently it's the answer."

And it *was* the answer, although not an easy one. When the project ended six months early, we were grateful that we hadn't uprooted our family.

Over the next few years, at different times, many things each of us wanted to happen, didn't. But inside our family, the code phrase would then emerge: "It's not what I prayed for exactly . . ."

Then, early one fall, Bill took a long-distance call. He turned to me, his voice holding the unnatural calm of deep fear. "Your father's been taken into surgery. There's severe heart damage."

Daddy? So ill? *Oh, dear God, please let him live*, I prayed as Bill rushed me to the airport.

My mother said nothing when I walked into the hospital waiting room. We simply held each other silently. Sitting beside her, I prayed as I had never prayed before. *Please let him live.*

For three weeks, my mother and I kept our vigil. My father regained consciousness, and one morning he squeezed my hand. But though his heart stabilized, other problems developed.

Whenever I wasn't with my father or mother, I would sit in the hospital chapel. My prayer was always the same: *Please let Daddy live.*

Get-well cards arrived from everywhere. One evening, I got a card from Bill. I tore open the envelope. It was "our" card, with this message to me added inside: "Have faith in God's answer, darling."

My mother couldn't understand why I stood in her kitchen clutching a crumpled card, alternately laughing and crying. But what Bill had helped me realize was that I'd been praying all wrong.

The next morning, I sat quietly in the hospital chapel. *Dear God,* I prayed, *I know what I would like, But that may not*

be the best answer for Daddy. You love him, too. So now I
release him into your hands. Not my will, by your will be done.

During the next two weeks, Daddy's condition was up one day, down the next. Then, on my mother's birthday, October 24, he died. Bill arrived the next day with the children. "I didn't want Granddaddy to die," sobbed Andy. "Why did he die?"

I held him close and let him cry. Through the window, I could see the mountain and the crystal-blue sky. I thought of my beloved father and the years of helpless invalidism he might have had to endure. And with Bill's hand on my shoulder, I softly replied: "Apparently, it was the answer."

13
GrandJack Held On

I never knew my husband's grandfather, yet he touched me in a deep, personal way. Here's how Bill told me the story about GrandJack.

"Bill," cried Granny, her voice sounding strange over the long-distance wires. "I'm calling with bad news. It's GrandJack. He's had a stroke."

"A stroke!" My grip on the telephone tightened. "I'll be right over."

As I drove to the hospital in Oklahoma where my grandparents lived, my mind was whirling with disbelief: *GrandJack! A stroke? It couldn't be!*

He was such a great bear of a man, even at the age of seventy: six-feet-four with a barrel chest and well-muscled arms, and the same reddish hair I had inherited. His jaw jutted forward stubbornly, but it was a quiet stubbornness, one that some folks might call determination.

His visits had been the highlight of my boyhood summers. With a grin and a poke of his work-roughened finger, GrandJack would wake me in the cool mornings and, fishing poles in hand, we would scuffle barefooted to the lake.

We never talked much; GrandJack wasn't one to waste words. He taught me how to clean a fish more by having me watch than by explaining the procedure to me. That was GrandJack's way, to expect you to figure out things for yourself, his way of saying, "You can do almost anything if you put your mind to it."

Now this fine old man lay helpless in a hospital bed. Beneath the sheets, his great barrel chest hardly moved. Tubes and dripping bottles surrounded him.

But GrandJack's grit came from an abiding faith in God, and that faith soon showed itself. Although paralyzed on his right side, he began, within days, to try to regain movement. By now most of the family, including my father, was there with my grandparents. We watched as GrandJack stoically tried to build on the slight movement he still had in the fingers of his right hand.

One morning my dad handed GrandJack a box. Inside was a baby's rubber football; just the right size to hold in your hand.

"Squeeze this," he told his father. "It will strengthen your fingers."

How GrandJack tried! Hour after hour, he squeezed that football. The effort made his face glisten with sweat. Yet slowly, as weeks went by, he began to get response, first in one finger, then in another.

"Look here, Billy," he cried proudly on one of my weekend visits. As I applauded, he slowly lifted his spoon and fed himself.

But a few months later, as GrandJack sat by the window in his wheelchair, he let out a small, hoarse cry. The rubber football rolled from his hand. By the time Granny reached him, he was slumped in his chair like a worn-out stuffed bear.

All his hard work was for nothing, I thought, when I visited the hospital. But I hadn't reckoned on the force of his spirit.

Though he couldn't talk, GrandJack gestured with his eyes. He wanted something. Puzzled queries from the family finally brought a shout of comprehension.

"You want your football!" I cried. "Is that it?"

A smile tugged at the corners of GrandJack's mouth. Carefully, I wrapped his right hand around the small rubber toy. The next day GrandJack left the hospital for home.

Days turned into weeks, and the Oklahoma prairie grass turned brown with summer's heat. GrandJack kept squeezing his rubber football. Though his speech remained slow and uneven, he reached a point, once again, where he could proudly lift a spoon and feed himself.

But then he had another stroke.

This time, when I reached the hospital, tears spilled from Granny's eyes. "How much more can he take?" she whispered. But once again, GrandJack fought back. Once again, the small football found its way into his right hand.

Autumn blustered into winter. GrandJack had a series of small strokes. He lay pale and wasted in his bed, unable to speak or to move. Yet to the very end, his eyes held the stubborn light of a fighter and his right hand loosely gasped the football.

When he died, two years after his first stroke, I had no chance to ask what happened to the toy football. But over the years, I thought of it occasionally — and remembered how GrandJack had never given up.

Twenty years passed. One spring, during an Easter visit from my parents, I mentioned GrandJack's football. As I related the tale to our teenage children, I felt tears well up in my eyes. "He never quit," I said. "Right to the end, he squeezed that toy football."

"I never knew it made such an impression," said my father. He seemed surprised.

At that moment, the telephone rang and the subject of GrandJack's football was lost in the ordinary events of the day.

The following year was a difficult one for our family. I had quit my corporate job to start my own business as an agricultural consultant. But the recession caused the market to tighten, and it began to look as if my business might fold.

Was it only coincidence that in the middle of these problems, when I was near despair, I received a small box in the mail with a note attached? "Dear Bill," I read in my father's scrawled handwriting. "I took GrandJack's football home with me after the funeral. Now seems the right time to pass it on."

For a few minutes, I couldn't speak. Carefully, I pulled from the tissue the small rubber football and set it on a corner of my desk.

For many long months I struggled to keep my business afloat. But there finally came a day when I knew the business was finished. Overwhelmed with grief and the bitter gall of failure, I sat alone at my desk.

A narrow beam of sunlight filtered through the slatted blinds from the window. The light came to rest on GrandJack's football. I stared at the small rubber toy, then picked it up and squeezed.

Suddenly, as if he were in the room, I seemed to hear GrandJack's voice: "Did you squeeze for all you were worth, Billy?"

The question hung in my mind. Had I? "Yes!" I whispered. "Yes! I squeezed the football as long as I was able."

And then — did the words come from myself, or from Someone else? — "No one can do any more."

That's when I cried, but now the tears were healthy ones. The sense of failure was gone, replaced by a sense of God's peace. I had tried my best — I had truly squeezed for all I was worth. No one can do any more.

There is a rhythm to our lives, and bad times yield to good. My business failure led me into another business that has enjoyed success. Our lives smoothed out.

Then one day we learned that Margery, a dear friend who had gone through surgery for cancer a year ago, was back in the hospital.

The February day was as gray as my spirits when I walked into Margery's room. She lay against the pillows, her skin pale, her eyes cloudy with pain. Her voice held the whisper of defeat.

"I fought back before, but this time . . ." The whisper faded and a chill ran through me. She was giving up.

"Margery," I said, reaching for her hand, "I want to pass something on to you." From my coat pocket I pulled out GrandJack's football. I told her the story of the brave old man who refused to quit. "I'm convinced God gives a special grace to those who keep on trying. Promise me you'll squeeze the football."

For the first time since coming into her room, I saw a small light in her eyes. She smiled. And squeezed.

Margery died eight weeks later. But I have it on good authority that she squeezed the football to the very end. No one can do any more.

14
Zigzag Faith

I've never liked what I call "ledges with edges." You know, those narrow paths with a sheer drop-off on one side. I don't like to drive over twisty mountain roads, or ski down narrow runs, or hike up trails that edge a cliff. Give me room, lotsa room, is my motto.

I wasn't thinking about narrow ledges, though, the day Bill and I started our October hike. The Colorado mountains near Aspen were covered in gold — the famous aspen leaves that shimmer and sway like a field of golden wheat during that time of year. A time of year that helps rejuvenate the mind, body, and soul.

We'd flown to Aspen on an impulse, both of us looking for a break in our two hectic schedules. I wanted more than exercise, though: I wanted some thinking space.

For months, I'd been wrestling with a desire to try a new path in life. My job at Hallmark Cards was secure and paid well, but it no longer fulfilled me. I wanted to try something different. But I'd have to step out in faith and I was scared, financially.

We started up a popular trail leading to Cathedral Lake. Neither Bill nor I had been there, but we heard it was beautiful. As I trudged behind Bill, feeling the weight of my knapsack, and the pleasant warmth of the beautiful day, I tried to let go of the weight of my fear. I wasn't having much luck.

Our trail wound through aspen groves, then along a rushing mountain stream. Magpies flitted in tree branches, their raucous calls blending with the water's roar. Gradually, the trail grew steeper, and I hunched forward, taking slow breaths.

We rounded a curve. That's when I gasped.

Our trail disappeared in a wide moraine of loose rocks —
"scree," mountaineers call it. Boulders of all sizes, torn loose in
some icy long-ago avalanche, dotted the side of the mountain.
To keep climbing, we had to follow a series of narrow
switchbacks that zigzagged through the scree, as if some hand
had carved the mark of Zorro repeatedly into the mountainside.

Bill pulled out his topographical map, while I peered over
his shoulder. "Once we climb through this, we'll reach an
alpine meadow and the lake. We can eat lunch there."

"*If* we reach it," I said doubtfully. The ledges looked
awfully narrow. But I hated to seem like a wimp, so, gingerly, I
picked my way across the loose rocks behind Bill. A breeze
brushed my face; otherwise, except for the click of our boots
against stone, there was only that peculiar crystal-clear silence
that is part of high altitudes.

Bill led the way. Each switchback was just wide enough
for me to place one foot after another, Indian-style. I
concentrated on keeping my balance, trying not to look over the
edge or think how easily I could slip and fall.

We reached the seventh turn. "Only two to go," said Bill,
cheerfully. Suddenly, I stumbled. My foot slid, and I grabbed
frantically at empty air. "You're okay!" shouted Bill. His
fingers clutched mine and held tightly until I regained my
balance. My lungs burned, not from exertion but from panic. I
felt like someone trapped on the outside ledge of a tall
skyscraper. "Bill," I whispered, "I'm afraid." He backed down
to where I stood. "We're almost to the top, Barb. You can make
it."

I hardly heard him. My mind was frozen on one sentence,
repeating it over and over: *Don't move. Don't move. Don't
move.* Even bending my fingers frightened me, as if the
slightest shift might send me plummeting down among the
rocks. When a gust of wind tugged at my windbreaker, I
whimpered but told myself not to panic at the thought that the

wind might knock me off the ledge. A pebble ricocheted down the mountain. It sounded like a gunshot. Then Bill's voice was at my ear. "Barb, honey, right above us, the trail widens into a gorgeous meadow. I checked it out. Just two more turns. You can do it."

I took a frightened step forward — only because two turns up seemed better than seven down. Hardly breathing, I inched my way along, while Bill talked me through one turn . . . then another. Finally, he shouted, "You made it!" Sure enough, the trail widened. I grabbed the comforting branch of a pine tree.

We passed through the shadow of some pines and emerged into sunlight, and a wide, lush alpine meadow. Scattered wildflowers could still be glimpsed, and where there weren't flowers, tall waving grass, in autumn gold, stirred like wheat. Cutting through the meadow was a tinkling stream that ended in a crystal-clear lake.

The October sun warmed our skin and we dropped our packs to run, joyously, across the meadow, falling, at last, onto the grass, which felt like a soft feather bed. We stretched out in the sun, our heads pillowed on our backpacks, and snoozed. Then, sitting up, we ate, with gusto, our peanut-butter sandwiches and crisp apples, washing our food down with good cold water out of our canteens.

"Let's explore," suggested Bill, and I followed him, eagerly now, because the terrain was so wide and so easy to navigate. Yet in the back of my mind, even as we laughed and climbed, I felt the nugget of fear: *We'd have to start down the mountain eventually. How would I ever do it?* Just thinking about the switchbacks sent adrenalin pulsing.

Too soon, Bill looked at his watch. "It's four o'clock, Barb."

"I know."

"Time to start down."

"I know."

We pulled on our packs for the descent. The sky, cloudless until now, had turned gray. Ordinarily, I wasn't afraid of afternoon storms — they're common in the mountains, and we carried rain ponchos — but as I thought about the ledges, slippery with rain, my stomach turned even more queasy.

I began to pray, an inarticulate prayer at first, hardly words at all, more just a feeling of, "Lord, I'm afraid." As we got closer to the steep edge, my breath quickened and so did my prayer.

We reached the top of the switchback. It hadn't begun to rain yet, but cool wind tugged at our sleeves, and gusted against the rocks. "I'll go first," Bill offered, "and talk you down." I suddenly sensed that he was more worried than he let on. He was afraid I might panic midway and freeze.

He's got good reason to worry, I thought. As I looked over the edge at the rocky moraine, my whole body grew weak. My heart had turned into a wild thing, a captured bird slamming madly against the walls of its cage. *I can't do it,* I told myself. *They'll have to come get me by helicopter.*

"Ready?" coaxed Bill.

I shook my head and stood very still. If I ever hoped to get down this mountain, I needed more than Bill's help. I closed my eyes and felt my prayer, no words at first, just that feeling again, of fear. *Oh, God, I'm so afraid*. Then, I thought of Jesus, and how terrified His apostles had been in their boat. They had called on Jesus to quiet the storm. I could, too. I held out my hand, and as I did, the wind seemed to soften. Was it my imagination, or did I really feel a slight pressure on my outstretched fingers?

Slowly, keeping my eyes focused on each step I took, I began edging down. I held out my hand, as if I were holding the hand of someone walking beside me. As I walked, I talked. My words ran together. "Thank you for walking with me, Jesus. I know you won't let me slip. I know you're here with me, I can feel it, thank you . . . There! We made the first turn . . . keep holding my hand, and walk on the outside, please . . . I know you won't let me fall. Thank you, Jesus, thank you . . . Here's the second turn . . ."

Step by step, I inched my way down all nine zigzags. Only when I reached the last ledge did I dare lift my eyes from my feet.

Bill scampered down behind me and gave me a hug. "Barb, you did it! You conquered your fear. Look what you came down!"

I looked up the steep slope and laughed giddily. "I did do it, didn't I? But not alone. I had help, Bill." I told him how I'd prayed and pictured Jesus, walking at my side. "And, believe me," I laughed, "I pictured Him walking on the outside!"

The rest of our hike down seemed tame. As we reentered the aspen groves, I thought how scared I was to venture out. Hadn't I learned today that inside I had what it takes to maneuver a difficult path? Fear paralyzed me until I trusted in God's power. If I could manage those zigzags with the help of prayer (and Jesus Christ), why not other parts of my life?

I thought of something else. I would have missed all the beauty of that high mountain meadow if I hadn't climbed through the scary zigzags. Did I want to miss more beauty in life, or the joy of creative fulfillment, because I lacked courage to climb scary paths?

That's when I made my decision. It was time to leave the safety of the corporation — time to strike out in a new direction.

I could hardly wait to get back to Kansas City.

15
Soul on Sabbatical

*Ever gone on retreat? Taken a few days off from the
day-to-day striving for success to sit in solitude and prayer? A
retreat is a true sabbatical for the soul . . . a way to refresh and
sometimes rediscover what matters most. Here is how I
experienced one such retreat.*

On a crisp, windy Friday in March, I pull up in front of
Conception Abbey, the sprawling Benedictine monastery
whose red brick towers rise three stories high above sleepy
farm country in Missouri.

A small sign bids "Come in. All are welcome here."
Father Philip's voice is like a smiling echo.

"Welcome!" he says, his black robe rustling as he guides
me into the visitors' parlor. A Benedictine monk for forty
years, Father Philip is the prefect of guests — my host.

There are always guests at the abbey. We come, each of
us, for a weekend or a week away from our very ordinary
worlds. We come, not with a group but on personal journeys of
our own.

For several years, I have been making such a journey once
or twice a year, making reservations with a quick phone call to
the abbey. I am not unusual. Personal retreats are becoming
popular among people of diverse religious denominations or no
denomination at all. Like a deep breath taken in the middle of a
long run, retreats offer a spiritual second wind.

Father Philip escorts me and other weekend guests to the
visitors' dining room, where we say aloud the blessing and
accept with thanks the wholesome, hearty food of the abbey.
(Though, with a smile, I notice that the monks do have a
microwave.)

Seated next to me is a woman about my age —
mid-thirties at the time — who explains she is thinking of
joining a religious community. "It would be quite a life-style
change," she admits. "Right now, I'm a medical director in a
hospital. I own a condo and a sports car. I've come to pray
about it."

A plump lady with corkscrew curls beams at me from
across the table. "Jacob and I came here every year for retreats.
Jacob did love his retreats." Her eyes darken. "I've come here a
lot since Jacob died. I feel close to him here."

A married couple from St. Louis hold hands beneath the
table. "We've never been on a retreat. Some friends suggested
it." Hesitantly, the wife adds, "We're Methodist, you know."

Father Philip chuckles. "Some of my best friends are."
Everyone laughs, even the taciturn, middle-aged man whose
only comment has been, "Pass the potatoes, please." Now he
adds, "I've come here to think."

The abbey is a good place to think — and pray — and
search one's soul.

After dinner, I walk to the monastery's church. It's tall
and cavernous and seems to whisper of God. In daylight,
sunbeams halo the stained-glass windows, but now there is only
a hushed, peaceful darkness. The solace of quiet steals over me.
It takes a while to come into relationship with God. It takes that
most rare commodity — long moments of silence into which
the soul can settle and grow attentive to the "small, quiet voice
of the Lord."

This is what a retreat offers most of all — hushed quiet in
prayerful places. As I kneel in the dark cathedral-like church, I
feel surrounded by the gentle spirits of all who have shared this
pew.

A small light, its beam no larger than a flashlight's glow,
suddenly blinks on behind the altar. Inside the sanctuary,
behind the free-standing altar are the monks' prayer stalls. They

file in for Vespers in their long-skirted habits, turning on small lights above each stall. High overhead the church bells peal. "Hosanna!" cry the bells. "Come and worship!"

The monks sing the evening psalm in English, but in the cadence of a Gregorian chant: "Bless the Lord, my soul! Lord God, how great you are."

And from the other line of prayer stalls, an answer: "Clothed in majesty and glory, wrapped in light as in a robe."

Back and forth go the ageless words, rising and falling in minor key melody. As I listen, I feel part of this psalm and all the psalms that have been sung since David's time. It is a timelessness that stretches over centuries, a wellspring that touches all who take part in Judaeo-Christian worship.

In the morning, I rise before dawn to join the monks for morning praise. How I love walking through the predawn darkness! Behind me, only stars break the quiet country sky. In the distance, a rooster crows. A cow moos. Ahead lies the shadowed church steeple. I watch window lights flicker on, one by one, inside the monastery residence. A soft noise beside me announces a monk already on his way to church. We nod but do not speak. In this place, silence is communication.

Later, I am met by the same silence as I leisurely stroll around the farm pond beyond the abbey, as I sit on one of the sloping pasture hills with spiritual books to read. And yet — wait! My ears now pick up a constant hum and twit and rustling. A dragonfly zooms past. A hummingbird hovers. Bees murmur. Cicadas tune up their stringed orchestra.

Sun warms my city skin. I smell the hollyhocks. I grow aware of a miniature world in motion at my feet. Tiny ants, a slow-moving beetle, a spider at work between two tall grass blades.

Out in the fields, a cow moos again. A tractor churns.

My eyes lift from the scurrying insects to the far horizon, and a joy explodes within me, a sense of oneness with our world. For a moment — just a moment — I am not alone, a creature trapped inside skin and mind. For a moment I am one with all God's creation, one with the trees and the insects and the March wind that stirs the pages of my book, with the clouds and the birds and the seas beyond the horizon and the animals and people that inhabit our planet. For a moment — just a moment — I sense how all souls touch, each a part of the whole, and the whole is the grandeur of God.

The moment passes, but its memory lingers and puts into perspective my everyday groans and petty dissatisfaction.

I have felt a glorious appreciation of God's world while fishing or hiking in the Colorado mountains . . . but it is not the same. Then I am like a viewer who sees a beautiful painting but who is outside the experience, only a viewer. On retreat it's as if I become one with that painting as I feel and momentarily am the artist's brushstroke. And the artist is God.

I think this sense of oneness comes because on retreat we can step outside our day-to-day time frame to focus, not just on relaxation or unwinding but on our relationship with God. On retreat, God is not a by-product. A retreat is like William Blake's poem come to life:

> *I give you the end*
> *of a golden string.*
> *Only wind it into a ball.*
> *It will lead you in*
> *at heaven's gate,*
> *Built in Jerusalem's wall.*

A retreat offers the time and space and silence to follow that golden string.

Sometimes I choose a guided personal retreat. Then I meet with a monk and we set a spiritual goal. He assigns me biblical passages relevant to my needs and we meet and discuss. For some, especially first-timers, a guided retreat is needed. It is not easy to dwell alone with God for long unstructured hours. When we're not used to it, it can even be frightening. *What do I say?* we wonder.

But there is another aspect to retreats. Others who come are also searching for "heaven's gate," and though we may come together only for meals or through an unplanned meeting on a pathway, I have frequently gained a new insight from someone else's experiences in encountering God.

The taciturn, middle-aged man I met at supper turned out to be a plant manager who was confronting a tough career decision: Should he go along with his boss on some shady practices that by-passed federal safety standards? Or should he refuse and possibly get fired?

"I came here to think . . . and talk it over with God," he confessed on the Sunday we both planned to leave. "And I've decided to do what I know is right." For the first time his face looked relaxed. "This weekend has reminded me that faith in God means you've got to be willing to trust. It's easy to forget that when you're sitting in the middle of a noisy factory."

"It's easy to forget, period," I replied. And thought again of the golden string. Truly, a retreat gives time and space to wind our string into a ball and — at least for myself — let us discover "Jerusalem's wall."

16
One-Minute Prayer

Remember the book *The One-Minute Manager*? It hit bookshelves with a small explosion. Time-conscious managers loved it, since it provided practical tips to better management — in one-minute segments. I borrowed from that concept.

You see, though I start my day with an hour of prayer, what about all the rest of the day? "How can I stay aware?" I wondered. How can I practice the art of living prayerfully in the present moment?

Then I recalled *The One-Minute Manager*. Why not one-minute spirituality? After all, most of us feel the same time constraints managers feel on the job. But how can we become more God-conscious — in sixty-second bites?

I began to try some things, and asked other people for ideas. Here's what I came up with regarding prayer . . . one minute at a time. (You can probably add to this list with ideas of your own.)

Telephone thanksgiving ❦ I let the telephone's ring remind me of God's blessings. Every time it rings, I recall something good in my life and say a brief prayer of thanks.

Thirty-second eye contact ❦ Too often, we ignore the person we don't know. I began to make eye contact with people I met at the supermarket or mall, especially the clerks who served me. I looked in their eyes and for that moment, really *saw* them; almost always, I got a big smile in return.

Observe a green, growing thing ❦ Whether it's a tree, flower, or indoor potted plant, I really *looked* at the veins in the leaves; I counted the petals in a flower. To see for a moment one of God's beautiful creations helped me see my own place in the universe.

Stay in the present moment ❦ I knew I worried too much, and let my fears send me spiraling into the future — a future that seemed fraught with peril. So when I felt fear build in me, I took a deep breath and told myself to live, for one minute, in the present moment with God. After all, God gives us our lives moment by moment. It's the only way we can live. So I experienced God *now*.

Perform a one-minute kindness ❦ I used to feel guilty because I didn't work weekly in a soup kitchen or a hospital. But that's not possible for me. However, I do keep postcards handy, so I scrawl a quick note to a friend or older relative. I try to think of other quick kindnesses: letting a car in when the traffic lane narrows; lending a hand to scrape the ice off an older person's windshield; carrying a plate of cookies to a neighbor (even if they're store-bought).

The one-minute fast ❦ I'm a nervous eater, often tempted to eat something I shouldn't. I'm famous (or is it infamous?) for ice-cream binges! Now, when I'm tempted, I wait for one minute and offer the minute to God. I ask the Holy Spirit to help me control my eating desire. Often, by the time the minute is up, my temptation has passed. If it hasn't, I forgive myself!

Nightly affirmation ❦ As a recovering perfectionist, I can become far too critical of myself. So now I take a minute at night, look in the mirror, make eye contact with *me*, and repeat, "I am loved, and through Christ, I love," or "God loves me and I love me."

My miracle journal ❦ Miracles happen to us every day; sometimes we just don't notice! So I keep a MIRACLE JOURNAL and each night I write down one miracle that occurred on my day. My grandson's smile. A rainbow. An unexpected kindness I received. A serendipitous gift. It's a wonderful journal to thumb through when you're down.

A red-light act of contrition ❦ At every red light, I tell God I'm sorry for the times I stopped living in the Spirit and ask for grace to live His will now.

Taking a minute to listen to someone ❦ Sometimes it's a child, sometimes a spouse. Someone I can *really* listen to instead of absently saying, "Uh-huh."

The shower-power prayer ❦ Water is a powerful Christian symbol. As I soap and rinse myself in the shower, I pray to be cleansed from feelings of anger, resentment, and bitterness.

The alarm-clock prayer ❦ When my alarm goes off, I used to get up muttering. Now it's a reminder to repeat this from the psalms, "This is the day the Lord has made. I rejoice and am glad."

Lunch-box communion ❦ Over lunch, I spend a minute experiencing the act of eating. Not "eating and reading." Or "eating and talking." Instead, I eat slowly and notice the taste and texture of each bite and I thank God for our incredible abundance of food.

The count-to-sixty-and-stop-a-fight prayer ❦ Ever burst out in anger and regretted your words later? I have. One way I try to gain control of my tongue is to count to sixty this way: "One for God, two for God, three for God . . ."

Remember the God-holder prayer ❦ Everyone we meet is a God-holder. Especially when someone acts rudely or meanly, it helps me temper my response when I remember that God is in each person. Like candleholders, each of us holds the Divine Light (even if temporarily we hide it under a bushel).

The one-minute quick-change for God ❦ Let's face it: We all have habits that drive our spouse (child/friend/boss) crazy. And sometimes it's something little: like cracking our knuckles or forgetting to put the cap on the toothpaste or leaving lights on all over the house. My friend Don suggested I pick a habit that bothers someone else and dedicate one minute a day to correcting it. Do it in God's name. I was surprised how effective a minute can be, when it's used consistently.

The TV minute ❧ Commercials bug me, but now I use them to focus on the Christian call to live simply. I notice how few products advertised relate to what we *need*, and how many are designed to make us *want* what isn't necessary. I talk back to commercials, too.

The gas-pump minute ❧ As I pump gas into my car, I ask God to let the Holy Spirit flow into me, filling me with holy energy.

The peanut-butter prayer ❧ I don't do this one, but a friend of mine does. When making school lunches, she whispers a loving prayer into each lunch sack. Sometimes she adds a loving note, too.

The elevator blessing ❧ Notice how people always stare at the dial when riding in an elevator? Instead, I spend my elevator ride silently asking God's blessing on my fellow riders.

I wish I could say I do all these exercises consistently, but I don't. Yet when I remember, each one gives me a way to bring God consciously into my life for at least one minute. And what is life, after all, but all those minutes added up? Like the Buddha said, "Drop by drop, the cup fills up." In contemplating this, we Christians would do well to paraphrase it: "Minute by minute, prayer will change us."

Discovering Our Authentic Selves

Our life's work is defining ourselves.

Kierkegaard

Do you know who you *really* are?

I have a *Blip Theory*.

At seventeen, my daughter, Sony, won awards for a painting that hangs on our wall today. It was a fine painting, much better than anything else she'd created. I saw it as a blip. Like a bubble rising on the water, it gave Sony a glimpse of her full potential.

I think we all have blips. Bubbles of grace.

Recognize any blips in your life?

"On the one hand, we long for wholeness," says Harry Williams, dean of St. Paul's Cathedral in London, "but on the other hand, we're afraid of the very wholeness for which we long, and fight against its growth in us."

Becoming whole — authentic — true to our selves — calls for us to step out, to risk and walk the razor's edge. As the skin horse told the Velveteen Rabbit, it hurts to become *real*.

For years, I lived my life according to my parents' expectations, and was content . . . until life itself nudged me insistently. Until the "I" of I stirred within me, and then, I wrestled with it, just as Jacob wrestled with the angel.

Do you feel a nagging restlessness? It may be a sign of grace, calling you forward. "The wrath of God is the refusal to allow us to rest until we have become fully what we are," says Williams.

It's scary to pursue our blips. Psychologists say people back away because the pursuit requires discipline and inevitable suffering.

Of course, the truth is, *life* involves suffering. We can't escape it. Yet we try, by choosing the pain of neurotic escape over the authentic suffering of growth. I know this as only a grade-A genuine recovering neurotic can.

Neurotic pain comes from clinging to outmoded maps or beliefs. Subconsciously, we all create maps — or scripts — to guide our lives. M. Scott Peck describes those maps in his book *The Road Less Traveled*, and says pain comes from refusing to redraw our inner maps to fit current reality.

My friend Bob Kirkwood was a Navy fighter pilot in the late sixties. One morning, while on a six-month cruise to the Western Pacific, he looked in his shaving mirror. "I'm the thirty-five-year-old father of five children, and I'm in a twenty-one-year-old's job. What am I doing here?" Bob saw that he was living by an outdated map. A year later, he left the Navy, having recognized who he really was — a father longing to be home with his children.

Each of us must decide if we have the courage to "blip up" in life — and become all we have in us to be.

That's what the next experiences are about.

17
I Had Money and Success;
What Was Wrong?

You could feel it, hear it: the rich, swaying rhythm of several hundred dancers in the high open lobby of Kansas City's Hyatt Regency Hotel. Colored balloons floated gaily in the air while a number of relaxed and happy guests at the Friday afternoon tea dance stood on the lower of the three skywalks to watch the dancing.

Suddenly — a noise. Loud, like a firecracker. Then a peculiar instant hush, broken by screams.

"It's falling! It's falling!"

Four floors up, the forty-five-foot-high top skywalk had torn loose. Tons of concrete and flying bodies crashed with sickening force onto the crowded dance floor below. Terrified screams turned into moans . . .

No, I was not at the Hyatt that night. I had planned to go, but an advertising deadline kept me working late. Yet that disaster made me rethink my whole life.

At that time, in 1981, I was owner of a small but profitable advertising agency, earning more than sixty thousand dollars a year. Active in county politics, I was an elected trustee of our community college.

Fifteen years after John died, I was considered a "successful" woman. My staff was small (three plus free lancers), but our client list had grown rapidly in four years of business. "You've paid your dues," a business friend told me one day over lunch. He waved a piece of French bread in my ˈᵊᶜtion. "You can grow as big as any agency in town."

He could be right, I thought, as I drove back to my office. So why did the idea of building a bigger agency seem so unappealing?

A clue came a few weeks later when I sat in the warm California sunshine, reading a collection of short stories. It was my first vacation in months, the first chance I'd had to spend some time alone, with no deadlines and no personal demands to meet.

As I relaxed with my book, I felt an odd twinge — the kind of momentary sadness you feel when a song reminds you of a lost love affair. But I shook my head and forgot it.

Then came July and the hotel tragedy.

For weeks afterward, Kansas City was in shock. There was something incredibly personal about what had happened; everyone I knew seemed to know *someone* who had been there that night.

And what bothered us all was the tragedy's surrealism. If life could end so bizarrely at a tea dance in a major hotel — why, life could end anywhere, anytime.

"Makes you take stock, doesn't it?" said Bill, at dinner. "You know," he added, "there's a lot of living I still want to do, but if I died tomorrow, I can honestly say I feel good about where I am in life. I like the goals I'm pursuing."

"Not me!" I heard myself reply. The words were spontaneous, unexpected.

Suddenly, I knew that something very important was missing in my life. I heard these words so clearly, they might have been spoken aloud: "How did you forget how much you love to write?"

In an instant of clarity, I realized that in my pursuit of "success," I had placed my real dream on the shelf. The odd drift of sadness I had felt in California began to make some sense.

You see, I started writing stories in third grade. I still have some of them stuffed in a trunk in the basement. All through grade school and high school, I wrote stories; and in college, I earned my master's degree in creative writing. I planned to be a novelist.

But everyone knows you can't make a living as a writer. That's what everyone says, anyway. "Go into advertising or public relations," people told me. "That's where the money is. You can always write stories in your spare time."

So I went into advertising and here's what I observed: A hardworking, determined person will probably work hard and with much determination, whatever the job — and because of that — may succeed and do well. But he or she may never ask, "Is this the work I *really* want to do?"

I worked hard and succeeded in advertising, and because writing was involved, I persuaded myself for a long time that I was doing what I wanted to do. But now, it was as if my inner self had grabbed me by the scruff of the neck and shouted, "I won't be ignored! Pay attention!"

In his book *True to Experience*, English theologian Harry Williams described how Jesus calls us to repentance. "Repentance," wrote Williams, "means discovering that you have more to you than you dreamt or knew; becoming bored with being only a quarter of what you are, and taking the risk of surrendering to the whole, thus finding more abundant life . . . richer and deeper and more satisfying."

In the Hyatt tragedy I heard the call described by Williams.

When I told Bill about my feelings, he said, "You've always talked about writing a novel, Barb. But why can't you do it in your off-hours?"

I laughed. "*What* off-hours?" My business often took twelve to fourteen hours a day. Then came our three kids, my civic activities, the task of running a household, and a little social life. All I had left were bits and pieces of time. What I needed were some big hefty *chunks*.

Besides, something else was happening. The Hyatt, with its whispers of mortality, had forced me to reexamine my values. Somewhere, I realized, I had become caught up in the challenge of making money, in the idea that big is better, just because it's bigger, in the pursuit of success as defined by someone else.

One day soon after that, when I should have been writing a client proposal, I found myself staring at a fly buzzing along my windowpane. Idly, I drew circles on my yellow legal pad and realized, at last, how *bored* I was. I no longer wanted to write ad copy, client proposals, or brochures. I wanted to write for *me* — stories and magazine articles and a novel. And I wanted to do it *now*.

"But I'd be a fool to walk away from my business," I agonized. Besides, our family depended on my income.

And then there were my employees, Marge and Leslie. While Marge ran the office and production side, Leslie ably managed several accounts. Both were more than colleagues; they were close friends. I couldn't just close down and boot them out.

Yet if I didn't act, would I look back some day, an old lady with regrets, whispering to myself, "If only I had tried. . ."?

Momentous decisions are often triggered by minor events and that's what happened with me. I was stopped at a red light on my way to a client meeting when I saw a bumper sticker on the car in front of me. It said, "You can't cross a chasm in half steps."

Of course! It was speaking to me, telling me, "Time to take a *leap*." A leap of faith.

That evening, I pulled on my favorite old bathrobe, put Beethoven's Fifth on the stereo, set a pot of tea by my elbow, and while Bill was away at a meeting, I dug in with pencil and calculator to figure out how our family could get along if I stopped working for a year and simply wrote.

Eventually, I worked out a budget that I thought we could live with. *I* thought so; but would Bill? Money would be scarce. If the car broke down, we could be in trouble.

Also, I had to ask myself: *Would I feel comfortable, knowing that I was forcing our family to live on such a tight budget?* I'd always rejoiced that I could provide the extras — summer camp, ski trips, dinners out.

The kids surprised me. Andy and John shrugged. "Shoot, we can get along." Sony nodded. "I'm old enough to take care of myself." Bill seemed the most discomfited. But eventually, he, too, said, "Okay. Let's give it a try."

Talking to Marge and Leslie turned out to be harder. My palms were sweating when we sat down together at the office conference table. "I'm going to take a sabbatical to write full time," I announced nervously. They stared at me, astonished. "I know it sounds crazy," I stumbled on, "but I have to do it. I'll sell you the business or help you find other jobs."

Marge was the more upset of the two. All afternoon, as we discussed alternatives, she kept repeating, "You'll regret it. I know you'll regret it." I began to wonder: *Is she right?*

In the end, they opted to look for other jobs.

As Leslie cleared out her desk on her last day, my fingernails dug into my palms. Had I set wheels in motion I would one day regret?

But three days later, as I walked down the hall to my home office, a wild, free sensation swept over me. I have felt that way poised on sun-dazzled snow at the top of a ski slope. Free!

Mozart played on my stereo, while outside, cars drove noisily to work. I turned on my computer. I was alone but not lonely. Smiling, I typed the letters *C-h-a-p-t-e-r O-n-e.*

In the years since, I have published one book, written another, and seen many of my magazine articles in print. And I've also run into some answers I didn't expect.

Problems cropped up between Bill and me. In some respects, he was very supportive; but in subtle ways, he let me know just how much he missed my income. I had to fight pangs of guilt. Sometimes, the guilt turned into anger, and we wound up fighting. It was hard on our marriage.

When I stepped down from my position as a college trustee, I worried about losing community stature. Although I have lost some visibility, I learned something about myself: Stature lies within; it's not a reflection from outside.

Right away, I lost track of some people because my life no longer included business lunches. At first, I felt a pang; then I discovered a new world of writers who, like me, are struggling to publish, and we formed our own support network.

Most of all, I learned that once I made the commitment to pursue what I felt called to do, problems that seemed insurmountable had a way of solving themselves. Especially finances.

I began to ask just one question before buying anything: *Is this a life-or-death necessity?* Guess what? Almost nothing is! My spending dropped, but — and this is what amazed me — our standard of living stayed the same. That's when I realized how relentlessly our culture confuses *wants versus needs*; my "life or death" question cut through the confusion, and we were able to live comfortably on less.

I also discovered I could only do my "real writing" for four or five hours at a time, so I gave myself permission to occasionally do a commercial project that offered some offsetting income.

Though I've had some disappointments, I've never lost the joy I felt when I closed my business.

Have you heard a call? Perhaps as a disquieting urge now and then? Or a dream you put away on a shelf? It's God calling you, pulling you out of the comfortable — the familiar — onto the razor's edge. Perhaps you haven't heeded the call — but it has come, because it comes to each of us.

My friend Mary chose to stay married to a man whose chronic illness will eventually confine him to a wheelchair — and turn her into his caretaker. She consciously chose this option, even though some of her family urged her to leave him. "He didn't choose his illness," she said simply, "but I can choose my response to it." Harry Williams would say: She's found within herself "more than she dreamt or knew."

Chuck, a forty-two-year-old Trappist monk I know, left the monastery last year because he felt called to pursue ministry in a different way. His was a call to leave; Mary's was a call to stay.

Maybe you're not yet ready to heed your call. Don't worry; we can only move at our own speed. We can only hear when we're ready to hear. God doesn't give up. Throughout our lives, He continuously speaks to us, urging us forward to become all we have in us to be.

In that *becoming*, we find our joy.

Believe me, I know.

18
The Power of Hercules

Hercules entered our lives one April Sunday as we picnicked in the park. Andy, my tow-headed eleven-year-old, found him.

I was pouring lemonade when I heard Andy's shout. He ran toward us, holding what looked like a long, crooked stick. Then the stick wriggled and my lemonade splashed across the picnic table.

"But Mom!" Andy cried. "It's only a garter snake. May I keep him? Please?"

My instinct was "No!" — but the look in Andy's eyes made me hesitate. He was the youngest of my three children and I worried about him. At four, he'd required surgery on his ears and subsequent speech therapy. A year later, his father died; the same year, doctors diagnosed learning disabilities. He still required a tutor for dyslexia, and like many kids with similar problems, he'd grown up feeling "dumb," even though he was quite intelligent.

"He has to grow into his own learning power," was the way one doctor put it.

Lonely children often gravitate to animals, I've heard, maybe because animals offer unconditional acceptance. From an early age, Andy possessed an affinity for animals. Growling dogs would wag their tails at his approach. Hissing cats would purr. But dogs and cats were not allowed in our apartment complex.

I looked from Andy's pleading eyes to the unblinking eyes of the snake. Its tongue flicked at me, and I shuddered.

"Where would you keep it?"

"In my aquarium. I'll put a lid on and never ever let it bother you, Mom." He held the striped black snake up to his face. "Please, Mom. Please?"

I'm still not sure why I said yes. But Hercules, as Andy named him with a flourish, came home with us.

Andy set to work at once, cleaning the twenty-gallon aquarium, lining it with rocks and dirt, setting a branch upright in one corner for Hercules to climb on, and installing a lightbulb for warmth.

I admired Andy's industry and, once Hercules was safely behind glass, I could even admire the long, striped snake. In the sunlight, his scales danced and glittered, the way sunlight will catch on a dragonfly's wing.

"He's not trying to sting you," said Andy, when I jerked back from Hercules' flicking tongue. "Snakes use their tongues to sense things around them."

To a boy with dyslexia, reading can be an excruciating task. Andy had never read for fun, even though his tutor told us he had overcome his early handicaps. But after Hercules' arrival, Andy checked out every book on snakes in the library. We were amazed at all he learned.

Even more amazing were the changes in Andy, especially after his sixth-grade teacher invited him to bring Hercules to school. Andy was smaller than most of his classmates, but I saw his shoulders straighten as he proudly carried the snake to school.

Hercules spent all spring in the classroom, under Andy's charge, and adapted well. Before long, Andy had only to stick his hand in the aquarium for Hercules to slither to his outstretched fingers and glide smoothly up his arm. On the playground, he looped gracefully around Andy's neck, basking in the warm Kansas sunshine, his tongue flicking Andy's cheek.

Hercules returned home when school ended, to be joined, for Andy's birthday, by a pair of boa constrictors Andy named Mabel and Sam.

The boas were young, about eighteen inches long, and beautifully mottled in rich shades of brown and tan.

"How do you know they're male and female?" I asked.

"I just know," said Andy confidently. "I'm going to put myself through college by selling baby boas."

College! I marveled again at the changes the snakes had wrought. Here was Andy, who had thought he was "dumb," suddenly talking about college.

As summer veered toward autumn, Herc became Andy's near-constant companion. Often, when Andy went out on his bicycle, Herc rode with him, sometimes wrapped around the handlebars, other times tucked into Andy's drawstring snake bag.

Early one Sunday in August a violent shriek pierced the air. Andy stood in the driveway, clutching Hercules. "Herc got spoked," he said with a trembling voice.

Somehow the snake bag had become tangled in Andy's bicycle spokes. The result was a punctured snake. Hercules lay unblinking after being wrapped frantically in black friction tape. For the next twenty-four hours, Andy watched and worried.

I'll never forget Dr. Guglielmino's surprise on Monday when he opened his door to a boy holding out a bandaged garter snake.

"W-will he die?" stammered the bereaved Andy.

The veterinarian coughed. "This is my, uh, first, uh, snake patient," he admitted, as he gingerly unwrapped, then rewrapped, the tape. "I think we should let nature take its course."

Hercules survived.

Seventh grade is a tough year for kids, and for shy, insecure Andy, starting junior high could have been a nightmare. But now there was a difference.

I remembered what Andy's teacher had told us on the last day of grade school: "Hercules has given Andy value in his own eyes. For the first time he has something no one else has — something others admire. That's a new feeling for Andy. A good feeling."

In seventh grade, too, the snakes provided him with a sense of self. The lonely boy of a year ago smiled now. He held his head high and stepped confidently into the crowded school hall, knowing that the other kids whispered of him, "He's the guy with the snakes."

The snakes were a regular part of our lives now. When Hercules disappeared from the bathroom one day, after Andy had let him out to exercise, the whole family pitched in for the snake hunt. We found him in the closet, cozily wrapped around one of Andy's sneakers.

And we all watched, fascinated, when Hercules shed his skin, slithering out with a smooth, fluid motion to leave behind the old skin perfectly intact, while his new scales glowed with youth and promise. Carefully Andy collected the old skin and placed it in the shoebox where he kept his valuables.

We never learned what sent Hercules into convulsions that spring. As far as we could tell, nothing had changed in his environment. But one Friday afternoon, Andy ran to me screaming, "Hurry! Something's wrong with Herc!"

Mabel and Sam lay quietly curled in their corner of the aquarium. But Hercules writhed and jumped. His tongue flailed the air wildly.

I grabbed my car keys while Andy wrestled Hercules into the snake bag. Herc thumped and twisted as though filled with evil spirits.

Dr. Guglielmino injected some cortisone, and it seemed to work. Gradually Hercules grew calmer. Andy gently stroked his snake, and slowly Hercules reached up and flicked Andy's cheek with his tongue. He flowed again into a graceful loop around Andy's neck.

For several weeks thereafter, Hercules seemed fine. But then the convulsions returned, and we raced to the vet's for another shot of cortisone. Once again, Hercules recovered.

But the third time was too much. Although the cortisone quieted the massive convulsion, it was apparent as we drove home that Hercules was dying. His long, lean body lay limp in Andy's lap. His scales, instead of catching the light, were clouded and gray.

He tried to lift his head as Andy stroked his back, but the effort was more than he could manage. His tongue flickered once, weakly, like a candle flame about to go out. And then he was still.

Tears rolled silently down Andy's cheeks. And mine.

It would be another year before Andy would blossom, seemingly overnight, into the six feet of linebacker's build that would carry him through high school. After graduation, he was accepted at the University of California at San Diego in their tough engineering school.

Andy never did raise baby boas, but Mabel and Sam stayed with us all through high school, bequeathed, at the end, to Andy's biology class. They never took the place of Hercules, though.

In Andy's top drawer, there remained a dried snakeskin. Before he left for his last year of college, I suggested it might be time to throw it out.

Andy looked at me in horror. "Don't you dare!"

He touched the skin gently. "Ol' Herc . . . he was sure one splendid snake, wasn't he?"

Yes, he was. He gave a shy, lonely boy the first intimation of all he was — and all he could be.

Ol' Herc . . . I thank you.

19
Love in Unexpected Places

The doctor's diagnosis was clear — and left me heartsick. On the examining table Sony sat with her shoulders slumped, legs swinging, hair falling over her eyes. "Scoliosis is a spinal curvature," said Dr. Price. "But with a back brace we can keep hers from getting worse—"

"A back brace?" interrupted Sony. "But I already wear braces!" Her mouth glittered with silver wires, and more wires circled her head. The headgear looked like something from *Star Trek*. "For her overbite," the orthodontist had explained.

"Mom, I want to look like everybody else, not like the hunchback of Notre Dame!"

"You'll be out of the brace in a year of two," soothed the doctor. "By ninth grade for sure. And if you don't wear it . . ." He paused, then added, "Well, young lady, you could spend your life hunched over. Scoliosis is serious."

Sony jumped off the table and, glaring at both of us, spat out angrily: "I hate this place! I hate my school and the kids and the stupid wheat fields and how hot it is! I want to go back home to the beaches and my grandparents' house and — and . . ." Suddenly, she swallowed, and turned quickly, so we couldn't see her face. Only the trembling in her narrow shoulders gave away her tears.

I knew what else California meant to her. It meant her father. Three years had passed since he died, and still, she missed him. So did I. When I'd moved Sony and her brothers from San Diego to Kansas City, I moved them away from their grandparents and the neighborhood where people knew their daddy. I didn't realize what a difference it would make to them.

Defensively, I reminded myself: I have to support our family, and my job with Hallmark Cards is a good one.

But why must Sony face scoliosis on top of everything else?

We left the doctor's office, and I let her out at Hillcrest Junior High. I tried to be upbeat. "It won't be so bad, honey."

She scowled at me. "Yes, it will, Mom. But I won't wear this dumb headgear and a back brace, too."

Not waiting for a reply, she jumped out of the car and stalked up the walk. Two pretty blonde girls sauntered behind her, walking with the easy self-confidence of girls who belong. *Cheerleaders*! I muttered, and then wondered: *Will Sony ever feel she belongs here?*

It occurred to me, I could ask myself the same question. My co-workers at Hallmark were friendly. So was the couple who lived in the other half of our duplex. But I felt so lonely. I ached at night for John and yearned for his help in parenting. No one had warned me how tough it would be, juggling a job and three kids. I sighed. Maybe no one could warn you; maybe you had to find out for yourself. Like Sony, I felt as if my shoulders slumped from all the responsibility.

The cumbersome back brace arrived two weeks later. A white plastic girdle fit over Sony's hips. Aluminum spines, two up her front and two up her back, met at her neck. The round metal neckpiece pushed her head forward, like a turtle's head peering from its shell. "Mom?" said Sony. She had to turn her whole body to look at me.

"Yes, honey?"

"How dorky do I look? Really?"

I struggled for words of encouragement. Sony sighed. "Never mind, Mom."

"But—"

"I'll be okay."

"Hey, I'm supposed to prop you up, not vice versa."

"More propping I don't need."

We laughed at her small joke, the kind of laugh that's not far from tears. Carefully, like someone balancing books on her head, Sony walked downstairs to where her brothers wrangled over breakfast cereal.

"Wow!" exclaimed Andy. "You look strange."

"Thanks a lot."

"Aw, you look okay," said John. "If anyone laughs, just punch 'em out."

"Why not? A black eye won't make me look any weirder."

After John and Andy left for school, I watched Sony walk toward the junior high. She took small, jerky steps, awkwardly balancing herself. A group of older boys ran past, then turned, stared, and snickered. My fists clenched. I wanted to run out and do exactly what John advised — go "punch 'em out!" But I could only stay at the window, watching, while Sony trudged on.

Hip-hugger jeans were in fashion that year, but Sony had to wear oversized jeans to accommodate her brace. They bagged around her waist and ankles, while metal screws from the spines ate holes in the front of her T-shirts. "I couldn't look any worse," she said. And though she refused to wear the orthodontic headgear, she still complained about "all that metal junk in my mouth." Her narrow face looked unnaturally solemn.

As September turned into October, my job grew more demanding, and more often than not, I didn't get home until six. I kept hoping to come home and find Sony giggling with a friend, but she was always alone, sitting stiffly at the kitchen table, doing her homework.

Every morning, she walked to school alone, stoically ignoring the gang of boys who rushed past her, practically pushing her out of their way.

A week before Halloween, as I made a costume for Andy, I said, trying to be casual, "Who are your friends, Sony? You never talk about anyone."

"Well, gee, Mom, there are just so many, I can't remember them all." She pushed herself awkwardly out of her straight-backed chair — first her head, then the rest of her body, as if each were separate, pulled by invisible puppet strings. "Believe me, if I ever do get a friend, you'll be the first to know!"

Her bedroom door slammed.

Andy peered through the eye-holes I'd cut in a sheet as he asked, "How come she's so mad, Mom?" In reply, I merely sighed.

John met me at the door a few weeks later. He looked worried. "Mom, Sony's bawling in her room. She's been there all afternoon."

I ran upstairs. Sony lay sprawled across her bed, the back brace off and lying on its side as if she'd hurled it across the room.

"Honey, what's wrong?"

She turned her head to the wall. When I sat down beside her and touched her arm, she flinched as if my touch burned.

For awhile, I simply sat beside her. Outside, I heard cars pull up in driveways, the usual coming-home sounds in our neighborhood. Gradually, Sony's sobs drifted into hiccups, until she sat up, her eyes red and swollen.

"I fell down in the hall today."

"Oh, honey! Are you hurt?"

"In a way." She didn't look at me, just spoke in a flat gray tone. But as she talked, I could picture the school hallway, neon-lit, crowded and noisy between classes. Girls strolling, holding their binders in front of them, boys jostling, poking each other. Voices echoing against the red brick walls.

As she pulled books from her locker, Sony related, she realized she was late for her next class. She dreaded walking late into a classroom, so she hurried, and didn't see the corduroy-covered leg stuck out in front of her. She lost her balance, and her arms clutched at the air. The back brace was a heavy weight pulling her down and she fell, landing with a painful thud on her back.

Above her head came mocking laughter, then a male voice dripping with sarcasm: "Hey, whatcha doing down there? Mopping the floor?"

More laughter, while Sony struggled to roll herself over. It seemed forever before the bell rang and the hall emptied and she could pull herself up.

"Mom, I was like some beetle on its back, with its legs waving in the air! And everyone laughed. They laughed at me!"

"A few kids, honey. Not everyone."

Her look said as clearly as words, *Mom, it doesn't matter if it's just one.*

Seventh graders had to take home economics, and in November, they learned to sew by making stuffed animals. As Sony cut out a green cotton alligator, biting her lip in concentration, she heard a voice say softly, "That looks as dorky as you." At first, the words didn't register. Then she heard again, "What d'ya say, Dork?" Startled, Sony looked up. A girl named Lila laughed as she sauntered to her own place at the next table, where a group of girls — Lila's clique — giggled and whispered to one another.

The next day, Sony's scissors were missing from her sewing basket. "Gee, *Dork*, what a shame," said Lila. The group around her giggled.

"Did you take them?" demanded Sony.

"Who? Me?" Lila rolled her eyes, and, like birds twittering, her friends laughed.

The home ec teacher was no help. "Unless you can prove someone took them, dear, you'll have to get new scissors."

The teasing didn't stop in sewing class. As she walked up the school's front steps on Friday, Sony heard her name called.

She could never turn just her head; like a ship shifting slowly in the water, she had to turn her entire body. Lila grinned maliciously. "Oh, never mind, Dork."

Sony flushed. An hour later, she picked up her basket in sewing class and reached in for her alligator — all finished except for the stuffing. But the basket was empty. Frantically, she looked again. Then she saw Lila, smothering a laugh, and at the same time, spied a scrap of green in the scrap box. With a sick feeling in her stomach, Sony pulled out more scraps. It was her alligator cut into pieces!

"Oh, dear," said her teacher, "that's is too bad."

"Is that *all* she said?" I cried as Sony told me the story that night.

Sony shrugged. "I think Lila scares her."

My cheeks burned. "I'll call the principal tomorrow. Those girls won't get away with this!"

"Mom, no! You'll only make things worse."

"But why would that girl do something so cruel?"

"Because I look weird, that's why."

I'd never heard Sony sound bitter before. She was usually a gentle, good-natured girl. I wanted to reach out and hug her, hug away the hurt; but I couldn't even do that because her back brace wouldn't let me get close to her.

"Don't get involved, Mom. *Please!*" she repeated.

Reluctantly, I agreed. But I wondered if I'd made a mistake moving my children to Kansas City, even if I did have a good job. Would it help to transfer Sony to a private school?

I decided to talk to her after Christmas.

I took vacation, too, when the kids' school let out. "It's so good to be home," said Sony, happily. We played Christmas music, and baked Christmas cookies, and soon the kitchen smelled of cinnamon and nutmeg.

"Just like always," grinned John as he painted a sugar-cookie Santa. I was relieved when no one added, "Except that Daddy's not here."

When I saw the sign for the tree farm, I said to the kids, "Let's go. We'll make a new tradition, chopping our own tree." Pines dotted the rolling hills as we turned down a rutted dirt road that ended in a clearing thick with trees. "Race ya!" cried Andy, as the boys tumbled from the van. Slowly, more awkwardly, Sony climbed out. Like red-jacketed tornados, the boys circled trees, yelling, "This one!" and a minute later, "No, this one!" It took most of the afternoon before the kids agreed on which tree they wanted.

I was doubtful about the one they chose and said, "It looks awfully big to me."

"Aw, Mom, we want a big tree," argued John. He looked so expectant that I gave in, trying not to put a damper on the occasion.

But when we tried to stand the tree up inside our house, it wouldn't fit. "It's your fault," Andy accused John, who shot back with, "You helped pick it, dummy!"

"Boys, stop!" I intervened as I took a deep breath. "Sony, get the saw from the basement." It took awhile to saw the trunk and some lower branches, but finally, I hoisted the tree into the tree stand and it fit. "Look!" I said proudly.

But a groan came from the other side of the living room, "Mom, you butchered it!"

Like a man with a long, skinny neck, the tree's scrawny trunk stood clearly exposed. A gaping hole in the branches appeared where I'd cut too many off.

"Maybe if we turn the hole toward the wall. . . ?" It didn't work.

"How about hanging extra tinsel?" asked Andy.

We contemplated tinsel. Nope.

"The tree's *ugly*," said John.

"You're right," I agreed. "Let's go buy a tree at the tree lot."

"No!" said Sony. She stood gawkily in the middle of our living room. Her hair, as usual, fell around her face, and her teeth bit into her lower lip. "It was beautiful in the forest. It's not fair to get rid of it now."

I looked at my daughter's small, serious face. An odd silence hung in our living room.

"Let's keep it!" suggested John.

"Yeah," said Andy. "I'll get the tinsel."

So, as Christmas music played, we decorated our homely tree. Ornaments couldn't hide the hole, and Andy's extra tinsel made it look like a shiny boat listing sideways. "It won't win a prize," admitted Sony.

Yet we felt something *special*, a kind of protectiveness, about our tree.

When my neighbor brought us some pumpkin bread, her five-year-old daughter Emily stood solemnly in front of our tree, and for a long moment, said nothing. Then she looked at John and stated matter-of-factly, "That's the ugliest Christmas tree I've ever seen."

"Emily!" cried her horrified mother. But John grinned. "Yeah, we know."

On Christmas Eve, we turned out all but the tree lights. "It doesn't look ugly any more," murmured Sony in the soft darkness. She had taken off her brace and leaned against me.

"I love this tree," said John.

"Great tinsel," chimed in Andy.

"Love makes anything beautiful," I said and realized how true that was.

As I watched Sony start for school on January 2, her steps still stiff and jerky, I realized I hadn't talked to her about changing schools. But when I came home from work, she met me at the door, grinning broadly. Her braces glinted. "Guess what? Lila's not going to bother me any more."

"Why not?"

"I saw her after school, and she was alone, so I walked up, grabbed her arm, and said brace or no brace, I'd punch her out if she ever bothered me again."

"Yay!" yelled John.

I laughed. Sony did, too. We laughed so hard we had to prop each other up.

A few weeks later, Sony asked if I would drive her to Rachel's house.

"Rachel?"

"She's in my math class and we started talking. She's new, too, and guess what? She had to wear one of these dumb things last year."

I smiled at my daughter. How pretty she looked, with her eyes sparkling and her face animated.

Sony took off her brace in ninth grade. By then, she'd become a chattering happy high-school student with a warm group of friends. Today, she's grown and a mother herself. Every Christmas, she tells her two boys the story of our ugly Christmas tree. Always, she ends by saying softly, "What that funny tree taught me is this: Anything is beautiful if you see it with love."

20
Leap Into the Light

It's seven o'clock on a hot August morning, and sunlight trickles through the bedroom blinds of our suburban home. I wake up, knowing a full day's agenda waits in my advertising office. But something's wrong. I'm so tired. Like trying to run underwater. Everything seems gray, murky. A weary weight presses me down. What's happening? Now, behind my eyes, I feel another weight. Tears. Running into my ears, my mouth. So surprised. Why am I crying? Angry at the tears. *Come on, get up.* But I can't. I'm afraid. My skin feels funny, tight, like I've got a fever. And I'm so — overwhelmingly — tired. Fatigue rolls over me in waves. I can't breathe.

In our bathroom, the shower shuts off. My husband's face appears in the doorway. "Barbara, what's wrong?"

"I don't know," I whisper.

For months now, I have not been . . . my usual self. I've certainly had reason to feel sad. Mom's death from cancer came just two years after my father's, and it was hard, nursing her through her final agonizing days, full of anguish and seeming hopelessness. Then, in close succession, my father-in-law and mother-in-law died and Bill's company merged, costing him his job.

Still, those family tragedies are a year behind us and in other ways, it's a good time in our lives. Our children are happily grown. Our marriage is sound. Bill likes his new work in banking and my advertising business has done well. So why this despair I can't shake?

A few days later, I'm at my desk. So much to do. An ad campaign to write. But all I see on my yellow pad are large looping circles, aimlessly going around and around. Fear oozes through me and a voice whispers in my head, *You can't do it. You'll fail.*

Why am I so afraid?

The telephone rings. It's the marketing director at a local hospital I had hoped to get as an account. "We've decided to go with another firm," she says. My hand on the phone starts to shake. I watch it, as if it belongs to someone else. The shaking takes over my body. Now I'm rocking back and forth, weeping hysterically as if someone just died, and I can't stop. *I'll never work again. This proves it.*

Frightened at my thoughts, I open the phone book to SUICIDE HOT LINE. Fingers trembling, I dial the number, but when a voice answers, I hang up.

Somehow, I make it through the next few days. Then, late one afternoon, I drive down the freeway. Sun dances on the highway and sparkles on the hood of my car. My speedometer shows sixty. A freeway curve. Have to curve with it or I'll hit the abutment. My hands slip on the steering wheel . . . *Maybe . . . I should . . . just let go . . . no!* Something pulls me up short. I whip the wheel around, just in time!

Shaking now, I pull onto the shoulder. Got to breathe. But I can't. Help! I'm suffocating. Help! Unroll the window. Hot air blows in. Can't breathe. Ah, finally! Air in my lungs. But what is happening to me?

My panic attack on the freeway made me accept that something was wrong, very wrong. Despite the legitimate sorrows in my life, my feelings had gone beyond normal grief and worry. I was in alien territory.

When my friend Sarah phoned that afternoon, I confided in her. Sarah is a bouncy phys-ed teacher who's been a close friend for sixteen years. As I related my panic attack and the suicidal thoughts that preceded it, I expected her to be shocked.

Instead, there was a long silence, and then, to my surprise, Sarah told me she understood what I was feeling. "One day ten years ago," she said softly, "I found myself in the bathroom with a razor blade at my wrist. The only thing that stopped me was the sound of my kids arguing in our backyard."

I was flabbergasted. This had happened to cheerful, exuberant Sarah? Yet, as she described her experience, I heard an echo of my own thoughts and fears.

Sarah told me about Dr. Win Hall, the psychiatrist who had helped her, and urged me to seek professional help, too. It didn't take much encouragement. I called that afternoon and made an appointment.

I did something else. I purchased a small red notebook. On the first page I wrote in big letters: "THIS IS MY GET WELL BOOK, dedicated to my health and recovery." In that red notebook (the color red has always symbolized *hope* to me) I described my symptoms and later, my struggles to get well.

When I met Dr. Hall, I read from my notebook: "I feel hopeless, as if life has no meaning ✳ I feel like an abject failure ✳ Sadness overwhelms me ✳ I'm paralyzed by fear ✳ I can't make decisions, even though I've made decisions easily for years ✳ I'm weighed down by lethargy and fatigue ✳ I can't concentrate ✳ I'm overeating; who cares what I look like? ✳ I feel a heavy loss."

Dr. Hall smiled. Short, bald, and bespectacled, he looked more like a bank clerk than a psychiatrist. "You're a textbook case of depression," he said, and pulled out a prescription pad. "I'm going to prescribe an antidepressant to pull you out of that black hole you're in so we can talk about how you got there."

When I started to protest, he held up a hand. "Antidepressants aren't habit-forming. They merely replace chemicals your brain has stopped naturally producing. It's like insulin for a diabetic. You'll feel better in about three weeks."

I laughed. "What if I kill myself before they start working?" I meant it as a joke. Sort of. But he gave me his home phone number and made me promise to call — "day or night" — if I felt suicidal. Each year, I learned later, sixteen thousand suicides are attributed directly to depression, and the actual number is probably far higher. People who consider themselves tough or above human weakness — like police officers or doctors or ministers — are especially good candidates.

I didn't know it then, but I'd taken my first significant step to achieving wellness when *I admitted I was ill.* Depression is so insidious that most people ignore the symptoms, and family members often don't realize it's an illness. "Snap out of it," they say, or "Pull your chin up," or "Stop moping around." The depressed person tries. How many times had I pointed accusatory fingers at myself? *Weakling! Get going! Stop acting this way! Be thankful for your blessings!* But the angrier I got, the farther down I spiraled.

My daughter, Sony, a psychology major in college at the time, was astounded to learn, during a visit home that fall, how depressed I was. "Why didn't you tell me?" she demanded. Friends echoed my daughter. "Why didn't you call us?"

The truth is, I was ashamed to ask for help. Ours is such a take-charge, stiff-upper-lip society that depression made me feel like a moral weakling.

But as I read and learned more, it became easier to stop judging myself so harshly. "Depression warps your thinking until you no longer see your world in a rational way," explained Dr. Hall. Slowly, I began to understand that I wasn't to "blame" for feeling as I did; nor could I get well through willpower alone. In the psychiatrist's office, as street noises hummed outside, I also began to see how my desire to be *perfect* had made me susceptible to depression.

"Perfectionists set impossible standards — then blame themselves for not reaching them," said Dr. Hall. "When you have to be perfect, you're *addicted* to bad feelings about yourself."

"Isn't it good to set high goals?"

"Sure. But there's a difference between performing at your best and expecting perfection. Do you know a single human being who's perfect?"

I remembered something I'd learned as a child: *Only God is perfect.*

Had I been trying to play God?

Dr. Hall explained that I could change my perfectionism — and other negative feelings — by changing my thinking. With his help, I began to consciously observe my thoughts. When I caught myself in a negative thought, I learned to mentally holler "Stop!" and to replace the negative with a positive.

Now, when one of my creative ideas got turned down, instead of telling myself, "Well, that proves it; I'm no good," I substituted: "A single turndown doesn't mean anything. I've had lots of success with my ideas."

It's not easy to change the thinking habits of a lifetime, but slowly, I began to make headway.

I began to vigorously exercise, too — not for my body, but for my head! When you're depressed, what you want to do is curl into a ball and sleep, like a roly-poly bug.

Instead, I joined an aerobics class, and every time I jumped to the music, I pictured the fear oozing out of my body along with the sweat. I visualized the endorphins as little creatures wearing white hats, battling the black-hatted bad guys who'd taken over my brain. I cheered them on: *Go for it, guys!*

When I slid into depression, I'd begun to isolate myself without realizing it. I stopped going to professional meetings or returning phone calls. I told Bill I felt too tired to entertain; increasingly I withdrew from family and friends.

One Sunday morning in late September, I spied a small notice in our newspaper: EMOTIONS ANONYMOUS it read and gave a phone number. A matter-of-fact voice told me EA is a peer-support group modeled on AA's twelve-step program in which you admit you are powerless over your problem and turn your life over to a Higher Power — "to God as I know Him." The voice asked, "Would you like to attend a meeting?"

The following Sunday afternoon, I nervously joined a half dozen people in a church basement meeting room. I wondered: *Had I joined a group of crazies?* But they looked a lot like me: typical suburbanites. Tom, a balding middle-aged businessman, described his anxiety and how ashamed he felt "to be so weak." Jill, an at-home mother in her thirties, talked about her depression in words that echoed mine. Jamie, a young man with acne, spoke slowly about his chronic grayness of spirit.

At the end of the meeting, we recited a group motto: "Just for today I will adjust myself to what is and accept my family, my friends, my business and my circumstances *as they come*." According to the EA handbook, most people want to run the whole show. If only our arrangement would stay put and people do as we wish, we think everything would be fine.

The twelve-step way accepts life as it unfolds, moment by moment. When you live in the "now," you can't worry about the past or the future and that's how you let go of fear.

I drew strength from the stories I heard at EA meetings. When other people described their feelings, or nodded as I described mine, I realized I wasn't alone, or strange, or weak.

One fall morning, as the rest of our household slept, I sat down cross-legged on a floor pillow. Somewhere in the distance, I heard a train, its whistle a mournful *Oooooooooooo*. Outside my window, leaves ranging in color from pale gold to dark maroon clung to branches. I thought how often I clung to my ideas of what *"should be"* instead of trusting in God's *"what is."* I was like those leaves, refusing to let go.

I breathed deeply. Though I'd started my day with an hour of prayer for several years, encouraged by my friend Don Campbell, now I began the ancient practice of meditation. It was a different kind of prayer, a prayer without words.

At first my thoughts strayed into humdrum areas. The argument I'd had with Bill last night. Errands I needed to do. My general anxiety over managing the day. Yet gradually, as my breathing slowed, my erratic thoughts slowed, too, and I felt something new — something that touched me with the same slow warmth as the early morning sun. I hardly recognized it at first. It was peace. For the first time in months, I felt the calm, sure feeling of inner peace. When I saw a leaf drop from the tree, I smiled.

Maybe I could let go, too.

During my early morning time alone, I wrote regularly in my red GET WELL journal. Journalizing was my way of talking to myself; it helped clear my thinking. When I wrote down my negative thoughts and how I had revised them, I felt encouraged to do more.

As autumn turned into winter, the pages filled. Imperceptibly, winter passed. One day, the bare branches of the tree outside my window were suddenly alive with green buds.

The blackness I'd felt when I first met Dr. Hall had lightened. The antidepressant helped — for depression, I now understood, is a *physical* disease whose symptoms show up in thoughts and behavior. But exercise and morning meditation had also helped my body restore its own natural endorphins. The group support of EA had pulled me out of my self-imposed isolation.

It all came together one morning in early March. I woke to a cheerful bird call. Sun streamed through my window. As I lifted my head from the pillow, a verse from Psalms came to me: "This is the day the Lord has made. Rejoice and be glad." Then a new sound gurgled and splashed and leaped into my throat. *Laughter.* I laughed from the sheer joy of being alive. That's when I knew I had conquered my depression at last.

21
I'm a Recovering Perfectionist!

Out of my depression, there came an unexpected gift. I was able to say: "I'm a recovering perfectionist." Like a recovering alcoholic, I know I can never say, "I'm cured." But every morning I get up, look in the mirror, and say out loud, "You don't have to be perfect today."

Perfectionism is rampant in our society and has a lot in common with alcoholism:

✔ Both offer instant highs . . . and long-term lows.
✔ Both require more and more consumption to get the necessary high.
✔ Both divorce you from reality.
✔ Both are addictive.

The most important difference between the two is that society recognizes the danger of alcohol abuse. Not so the dangers of perfectionism.

If anything, in our success-driven culture, perfectionism has become an epidemic. Men and women are feverish in their determination to achieve in every sphere . . . perfectly. The perfect career. The perfect relationship. The perfect family. At first, the path to disabling perfectionism appears to be the path to achievement: Achievers are admired, emulated, fostered. Like the casual drinker who never dreams of becoming a drunk, the outstanding college grad who gets a prestigious position in the business world never dreams that a focus on achievement could lead to personal destruction.

The difference between healthy achievers and overachieving perfectionists? The psychologist who helped me deal with my own perfectionism put it this way: "You are addicted," he said, "to bad feelings about yourself."

Did it have something to do with being the oldest child, carrier of my parents' ambitions as well as their nervous uncertainty about child raising? Many firstborn children *are* perfectionists. As an Army brat who moved around a lot, I tried hard to be perfect; it was my way of being liked. Some children have a genetic predisposition; you can see it when they're toddlers. They want to arrange their lives "just so."

We perfectionists are like race cars with two speeds: zero and 120 MPH. We're often high achievers — but at a price; either we do everything perfectly or we call ourselves failures. There's no room for "second best" or for simply "doing your best." Silver medals don't count — only the gold.

Kathy Ormbsby, a star runner for North Carolina State University, ran from a track meet one day out to a freeway overpass and *jumped*. She's now paralyzed from the waist down. In a moving interview months later, she described how perfectionism had imposed such heavy pressure to win every race that even death became preferable.

A widely respected physician shocked our local community when he committed suicide. After his death, authorities learned he'd run up heavy debts. Friends speculated that he couldn't admit to a flaw in any area of his life, so he didn't know how to ask for help. He opted, instead, for death.

I admitted to my own perfectionism the way most addicts finally do: I hit bottom in my depression. Trapped in that dark tunnel, where I saw neither light nor hope, I had to face the truth in myself.

Dr. David Burns, author of *Feeling Good: The New Mood Therapy*, points out that many people who suffer depression are perfectionists; conversely, many, if not most, perfectionists will experience serious depression at some point in their lives. This is why it's important to become alert. It's time to quit saying, "I'm a perfectionist," as if it's something to boast about.

Here are six danger signs of perfectionism:

1. Perfectionists are results-driven, not process-driven. The work we do has no value in our eyes unless it achieves certain goals, but often those goals are unrealistically high.

2. Perfectionists live in a black-and-white world. It's all or nothing; we're either winners or losers. Do you hear yourself say, "I'm *always* failing tests" or "I *never* do well"? Those are perfectionist words. We give ourselves no points for trying.

3. Perfectionists fail to discriminate. We wash our cars or paint our toenails just as painstakingly as we might write a major report, raise our children, or love our spouses. And those toenails better look perfect! Eventually, we burn out.

4. No matter what mountain peaks perfectionists climb, we see another peak and say, "*That's* the mountain that matters." Our own mountains never count.

5. Perfectionists constantly compare. We can always find *someone* who is smarter, or earns more, or has a bigger house or thinner thighs.

6. Perfectionists constantly require a "fix." As soon as I earn one point, I have to earn another — not because the work involved is worth doing, but because I need the self-confidence. I won't believe I'm really okay unless I get a new win to convince me.

It's not easy to become a recovering perfectionist, I discovered. I had to change the thinking habits of a lifetime.

During my time of healing from depression, I went to church one wintry evening for a candlelight service. As I sat in prayer, the flickering candles seemed almost hypnotic, and an intense awareness took hold of me: In insisting on perfection, I was trying to become God! I'd refused to accept my own humanness. Yet if God loves me as I am, how could I refuse to do the same?

That moment was a turning point. Like an alcoholic who admits, "I am an alcoholic," and starts the twelve-step program, I saw what I needed to do.

I had to redefine *success*.

No longer do I look only at results. Instead, I ask myself: Have I done the best I can do *at this time*?

If the answer is yes, I call myself a success.

On my computer I taped a sign: "Facing writer's block? Lower your standards!"

Our culture, I notice, continues to push the idea of being perfect: Society judges not how hard you play the game but only whether you win. I'm learning to "just say no" to that idea.

When I catch myself falling into old habits of comparing, or putting myself down, or feeling bad because I see a mountain that looks better than the mountain I climbed, I holler, "Stop!" and pull out my new definition for success.

Perfectionists are always recovering, and I fight my craving every day. Looking in the mirror, I say, "You don't have to be perfect today," and turn myself over to God. And if I momentarily fall? Why, I brush myself off and say, "It's okay. Nobody's perfect . . . not even a recovering perfectionist!"

What's Really Important

It's better to have a rich soul than to be rich.
Olga Korbut

What if you were told, "You have six months to live"? How would you spend your time?

It's a great exercise to help us get in touch with what counts. We like to think we'll live forever, despite the contrary evidence.

I once read a news story about an outstanding young man, just twenty-two, killed in a tragic auto accident. "How sad," I said to a Jesuit priest I know. "He died before his time."

"No," came the response, "his lifespan was twenty-two years, that's all."

Oh.

A while later, on a flight from Tucson, I sat next to a rangy Oklahoma cowboy. "I keep a happy list," he drawled, and explained that he wrote down things that made him happy.

Like drinking cold milk straight from the carton. Or watching a hawk catch the wind on a sunny afternoon. Or pulling a trout from a rushing stream.

I smiled, and thought of my own "happies": Making snow angels when I was a kid. Giggling with a best friend. Feeling my grandson's sleepy hug. Watching a beautiful sunrise or sunset.

Funny how some people put promotions and houses and fancy cars on their happy list.

If you had six months to live, would you work longer hours to win the next promotion? Or would you spend more time with your family? Maybe repair an injured relationship?

Before you read the next stories, stop and ask yourself, *What's most important to me?* Write down your answers. Go ahead, do it. No one's watching. Let your thoughts flow. Then, put your happy list in a special place, and make sure you can find it again.

22
Good-bye to the Money-God

I used to worry about money a lot. Even though our family lived in the suburbs, on a *Leave It to Beaver* kind of street, feelings of financial insecurity dogged me. I felt especially anxious one February morning in the early 1980s, as I slid into a booth at a neighborhood restaurant.

"What's wrong, Barb?" asked my friend Don Campbell. I spilled out my financial woes. College and orthodontic bills for kids. The new washing machine we needed to buy. The cost of plane tickets to see my aging parents.

"I wish I had more faith," I said. Sighing, I added, "I'm like the rich young man in the Bible — only not as rich!"

Don chuckled and signaled to our waitress. The two of us had met on a business project but now were personal friends, and we had breakfast together once a month. We usually wound up talking about our spiritual journeys.

All around us, crockery and silverware clinked. Voices grew louder as the restaurant filled. "You have a lot of faith," Don said. "You put your faith in your bank balance, that's all."

I lifted one eyebrow quizzically.

"Where we put our faith," he went on, "that's where our god is."

I squirmed.

"Want to let go of your money-god?"

When I nodded, Don smiled. "It's easy. Stop holding on to your wallet."

That simply, he introduced me to a whole new way to think about money. I call it "grateful giving." He called it tithing. Instead of focusing on what you don't have, Don said, the idea is to say *thanks* for all you do have by sharing with those who have less.

"Some well-meaning people," explained Don, "urge tithing because they say you'll get back more than you give away. But that makes tithing an *investment*, not a thank-you. I give ten percent of my income to God to say thanks for all that God has given to me."

When I heard "ten percent," my coffee sloshed across the table. But that's exactly what tithing means: giving ten percent of one's income. "We can't afford that! Maybe when the kids are through college or when I get a raise or when Bill's business makes more money . . . ."

Don shook his head. "There's never a perfect time, Barb. You'll find out," he added with a smile, "that you do have enough. Once you stop focusing on what you lack, you'll start seeing all that you have."

Don told me he deposited ten percent of his earnings each month into a special bank account he called his *Thank-You Account.* Toward the end of each year, usually at Thanksgiving, the whole family — Don and his wife, Sally, and their two boys — gathered around their dining-room table to decide how to give away the money in their Thank-You Account. They gave some of it to their church and some to charities and some to needy individuals.

I left the restaurant in turmoil. I couldn't believe Don seriously expected me to start tithing when we had so many other expenses. Yet I couldn't get the idea out of my mind. Most of all, I couldn't forget: "Where you put your faith, that's where your god is." Did I really want to worship a money-god?

Finally, I spoke to my husband, Bill. To my surprise, he told me he thought it was a good idea. "We *do* have a lot to be grateful for," said Bill.

So the next month, I wrote the first check to our newly opened Thank-You Account. My fingers trembled. Maybe, I thought, I should wait a day or two before signing the check. Over the next two days, the fear that churned in my belly made

145

me realize just how dependent I was on the money-god. Couldn't I trust the one true God to see us through?

Finally, I signed the check. "Thank you, Lord," I whispered, as I drove to the bank. My check disappeared behind the teller's window, and I felt peaceful. I'd turned my back on the money-god.

But my money-god didn't let go so easily. Six weeks later, the president of the ad agency where I worked called me into his office. His voice was somber. "I'm sorry, Barbara, our business is down. I have to let you go."

I could only stare, shocked and frightened. No job? But we'd just enrolled one of our children in an expensive special school. He needed it. And how could this happen when I'd started tithing? Was this how God repaid my generosity?

My friend Don smiled sympathetically but shook his head when I related what had happened. "Remember, Barb, tithing isn't an investment. It's a way to say *thanks* for what we have, whether it's a lot or a little. If you think about it for a while, you'll realize how much you still have."

Gradually, I saw that Don was right. I had lost my job but I still had good health and a loving family. We lived in a comfortable neighborhood in a country where we often take our blessings for granted. I had talent and energy. Why, I had a lot to be thankful for!

A few days later, out of my first unemployment check, I wrote another check to our Thank-You Account.

In the many years since, I've continued to tithe. Losing my job turned out to be one of the best things that ever happened to me. I went to work for myself and discovered I love the independence.

I discovered something else: how freeing it is to live based on an attitude of "grateful giving." I no longer wrestle with the question that used to haunt me: *Can I afford to give?* Since I'm already committed to give ten percent, what's left is the joy — yes, and the fun! — of deciding where to spend our Thank-You Account. It's a little like gift-shopping without a budget.

And you know what? Don was right about something else: We've always had enough money. Sure, we've had financial ups and downs, but there's always been enough.

Every so often, the old money-god comes back to haunt me, and I'll feel a twitch of fear, especially when business gets slow. When that happens, I've learned to do this: I sit down at once and write a check to a good cause out of our Thank-You Account. It puts things back in perspective. I stop worrying about what we lack, and start noticing, again, all that we have.

23

The Splendid Joy of Living Simply

I've never forgotten a conversation I overheard in the gift department of one of our city's best retail stores. A handsome, well-dressed couple in their early fifties stood beside a display of beautiful — and expensive — Christmas china. The man turned to his wife and chuckled, "You know, now that we can afford a set of china we'd only use at Christmas, we're at the stage in life when we're getting rid of stuff."

He's right! To many people, material "things" become far less important as they grow older. After the glitz and greed of the 1980s, people began to take stock, to examine the special blessings of living more simply. It's good for the environment to stop wasting precious resources. And it's good for our economy to "stop maxing our credit cards," as one economist put it.

But there's another benefit to simpler living. It *feels* good. It offers freedom and spiritual growth. For some, it means freedom from worry over debt. For others, freedom to work at something they really love, even if it doesn't pay as much. In some households, it means freedom for a parent to stay home with small children.

Admiral Richard E. Byrd, after months alone in the barren Arctic, recorded in his journal, "I am learning . . . that a man can live profoundly without masses of things."

Bill and I decided to live on less — and like it! — so we could do something we really wanted to do: move to the mountains of Colorado.

I gave away our formal dining furniture, we stored the king-size bedroom set, I packed away much of our fine china and crystal, and we moved into our cozy mobile home on the bank of a Colorado river.

Bill's suits hung, unworn, in his closet, because all he needed were jeans and wool shirts. Instead of expensive dinner parties, we barbecued informally on our redwood deck, listening to the music of the river. For recreation, we hiked and biked. And I continually discovered how little we really needed to enjoy life.

When my cousin Diana visited, along with her husband, teen daughter, and in-laws, Diana and Paul popped a small tent in our yard; their daughter threw her sleeping bag down in the bedroom I turned into my writing studio; and the in-laws slept on our foldout sofa. So far, so good. But how, I worried, would we ever manage with seven people and just one bathroom? The in-laws smiled. "We raised six sons with only one bathroom. You stagger your showers, that's all." I realized then, it's only been in my generation that Americans take two bathrooms for granted.

Inside our mobile home, we're not burdened with a lot of upkeep, so I have more time to write. And Bill pursued his lifelong dream to become an Aspen ski instructor. Most of the one hundred sixty-two eager applicants were in their twenties and thirties, so what chance did a fifty-something Midwest Rotarian have? Well, dreams come true if you care enough, work hard enough, and make the necessary trade-offs. Of the forty instructors selected, the oldest was Bill.

What's most exciting is this: We're not alone in opting for simplicity. In affluent Redlands, California, Linda and Milan Hamilton have made a conscious effort for years to live as simply as possible. "We don't have a lot of furniture," she explains. "We use boxes a lot. We eat frugally and don't spend much on clothes." By reducing their overhead expenses, Linda is free to pursue her passion of working with the hungry and homeless. Her efforts over the past six years have raised two million dollars to feed the destitute.

In Winter Park, Florida, Bob Hague gave up a comfortable city government job, one that paid $42,000, so he could become a full-time competitive fisherman. He and his wife, Ann, simplified their lifestyle substantially so that Bob could follow his dream.

You don't have to move to a new location or change jobs or lower your income to practice simpler living. Living simply starts with an internal attitude, a new way of perceiving what's important. As theology professor and author Richard J. Foster wrote in *Celebration of Discipline*, "An attitude of simplicity sets us free to receive all that we have as gift — a gift we can then freely share with others."

My friend Gail lives in a million-dollar home in Aspen. Our trailer could fit inside her three-car garage! Yet we ski and hike together because despite her affluence, Gail and her husband don't live ostentatiously.

Living simply is an attitude, as easy to adopt as opening your hand instead of clutching at all the things you own.

The first step is learning to differentiate between needs and wants. Advertising has trained us to think we need flashier cars, electric can openers, and designer-label jeans.

We don't. Try this. Make a family decision that, for three months, you'll ask before you buy anything: "Is this a necessity or a want?" A necessity means food for sustenance or what fills the soul's deepest need, such as, for a musician, a musical instrument. A want is what we think we should have so we can keep up with our neighbors or create a certain image. For three months, buy only what you need. You'll discover how little you buy!

At the end of that time, make this assessment: *Has your basic living standard dropped?* Probably it hasn't, because most of us spend on wants, not necessities.

Stay alert to addictive consumption. I have a friend who is single and spends a large part of her paycheck on clothes. She's gone way beyond any basic need for wearing apparel, or even the human desire to adorn oneself. This particular friend buys clothes when she feels unhappy or lonely or insecure; for her, clothes-buying is an addiction.

Begin to think about shopping in a new way, and go into a store only when you know what you're going to buy. If you're accustomed to strolling the mall as a form of recreation, break your habit because that's when people spend spontaneously.

Since it's always easier to spend "plastic money," keep credit cards out of your wallet. People who get over their heads in debt and go to consumer-credit counseling for help are told to cut up their credit cards. I keep just one bank credit card, and it's only for travel and emergencies.

Giving up the credit-card habit is one of the hardest changes for any family to make, yet Betty and Tom Martin, a couple I know in Easton, Kansas, have *never* had a credit card. They do something very old-fashioned. "If we want an item," says Betty, "we save for it and pay cash."

A second step is to live on less than you make. Bill tells people, with a chuckle, "We live below our means."

University of Missouri economics professor Eugene Wagner, and his wife, Jane, an English professor, did just that. While their colleagues were buying larger homes, they stayed in their modest graduate-student apartment. "By living simply, we could indulge our passion for concerts, books, and summer travel," Wagner told me.

To live below your means, it's necessary to stop comparing with your neighbors. A friend who lives in San Diego wrote me a sad letter recently. My friend lost his wife a few years ago and is now a single parent — and a good one! — but last fall, he lost his job in a corporate merger. Though he tried to joke about it, I could tell he felt he was failing his kids because he's not keeping up with neighbors who fly their children to Disney World for Christmas or Hawaii for spring break.

I wanted to grab my friend by the shoulders, shake him hard, and say, "Don't you see? What you give your kids is more valuable! You give them your time!"

Once you decide to drop out of the competition for top-of-the-line cars, boats, or other status symbols, you'll discover something wonderful: You get along fine without them. And the people who count don't care if you have them. Some extraordinarily wealthy people have chosen to drive old, non-luxury cars: J. C. Hall, founder of Hallmark Cards, for instance, and Sam Walton, founder of Wal-Mart.

Begin the practice of giving things away. Richard Foster described his decision to give away something that meant a lot to him: his ten-speed bicycle. "My motive was selfish," said Foster. "I wanted to know the liberation that comes from this simple act of voluntary poverty."

The practice helps us learn how much we can do without. I gave away a large number of books before moving to Colorado and though I felt some pangs, I soon discovered I have all the books I need; only now, I check them out of the library.

My friend Di sadly shook her head. Her ninety-year-old mother-in-law had to enter a home for assisted living. "She has so much *stuff*," said Di. "I wish she had made gifts to her children and grandchildren of some of her belongings. A figurine from her Hummel collection to each grandchild or her good china to her daughter. Instead, relatives are picking out what they want as if they're at a garage sale. There's no meaning behind any of it."

The ability to give something away keeps us from becoming owned by our possessions. Some very wealthy friends in St. Louis have beautiful art objects in their home, but they worry so much about being robbed (even with a burglar system) that it's apparent their possessions have the upper hand!

If you're really serious about living based on an attitude of simplicity, try tithing — giving away ten percent of your income to your church and other good causes.

Learn to enjoy things without owning them. Not far from where we live, in Aspen, one home for sale has a price tag of twenty-five million dollars. Yet the wealthy come to the mountains for exactly the same reason Bill and I moved here: to hike and bike and ski in a spectacular natural setting, and the beauty is equally available to us all.

When I sit, on a summer's evening, beneath the dark, star-studded sky, I feel deeply the wonder of God and this universe — and that makes material possessions seem pretty unimportant. Do you live near the ocean? Or a river? Or the desert? Or fertile farmlands? It doesn't matter where; get in touch, on a regular basis, with nature. It helps keep life in perspective.

Also, get in the habit of visiting art museums. If you live near a university, keep track of the well-known speakers who come to campus, usually at no fee. Make a game of finding all the fun things there are to do in your community — for free. You'll be surprised how much you find!

Look for friends who share your values. It's not easy to "push against the river," even when we decide it's what we want to do. The acquisitive attitude is very strong in our society.

A. B. and Ann Conner, in Atlanta, Georgia, practice simplicity by living in a quasi-communal setting. Though A. B. attended a theological school, he went into the business world, where he became very successful. But "it just wasn't enough," he says. Now, he and Ann, a nurse, live near the inner city, and A. B. works with the homeless on a nonsalaried basis, something he can do because they share a home with eight others.

Ming Chen and his wife, Karen Schneider — along with their three daughters — live on only half his paycheck. They own an economical turn-of-the-century farmhouse in Seattle, grow their own vegetables, shop at thrift stores, and belong to The Network of Parents for Peace and Justice (PPJ), which has chapters around the country. PPJ members believe in raising children in a nonviolent, socially active, simple environment.

"It's hard to do in our culture," admits Karen. "You need people who believe as you do." PPJ families from Greater Seattle meet monthly for potlucks, and occasionally join in social action, like petitioning for the children's initiative in Washington, D.C., or caroling in soup kitchens.

I asked the Schneider-Chens if they ever tire of being so frugal. Do they chafe at driving a '76 VW bus? Do they ever want to break out and rent a video? Or stroll the mall? Would their daughters like designer-label jeans instead of recycled?

Their girls occasionally ask about getting a television set, says Karen, usually after they've spent the night at a friend's house. "We just say it's not what we do," says Ming. To the Schneider-Chens, their lifestyle is rich and rewarding — in every sense but money.

Have you ever learned a new word and then seemed to see it everywhere? Once you make a commitment to simpler living, you'll soon find others who feel as you do because you'll be ready to notice them.

In the 1980s, a popular bumper sticker read, "He who dies with the most toys, wins." Recently, I saw an updated version: "He who dies with the most toys — still dies."

The Jewish religion defines a person's wealth as a mixture of all that you have — your health, your family relationships, and yes, your possessions, but only as part of the whole.

The Christian religion (to paraphrase the Gospel of Matthew) says it this way: "What does it profit you if you gain the world but lose your soul?"

24
A Gift From the Woman in White

*Most of the stories in this book are from my life or a
member of my family's. But when I heard the following true
story from my friend Jim, I knew I had to write it. It appeared
in The Catholic Digest, and later in Reader's Digest, and
letters poured in. But many readers misunderstood the
message: They wrote, asking for the gift, not realizing the gift
was already theirs.*

*After you read the story, think about it: Do you have the
gift?*

Jim Castle was tired when he boarded his plane in
Cincinnati that Friday night in 1981. All week long, the
forty-five-year-old management consultant had put on a series
of business workshops. Now he sank gratefully into his aisle
seat, ready for the flight home to Kansas City.

More passengers entered — business travelers in rumpled
suits, teenagers in jeans, a harried mother juggling an infant.
The plane hummed with conversation, mixed with the sound of
carry-on baggage being stowed.

Then, suddenly, people fell silent. The quiet moved
slowly up the aisle like the invisible wake behind a boat.
What's happening? wondered Jim, and craned his head to see.
His mouth dropped open and he gasped.

Walking up the aisle were two nuns clad in simple white
habits bordered in blue. At once he recognized the familiar face
of one, the skin wrinkled, her eyes warmly intent — a face he'd
seen in newscasts and on the cover of *Time*.

The nuns halted, and Jim realized that his seat companion
was going to be Mother Teresa.

As the last few passengers settled in, Mother Teresa and her companion, who sat next to the window, pulled out rosaries. Each decade of the plastic beads was a different color, Jim noticed. The decades represented various areas of the world, Mother Teresa told him later, and added, "I pray for the poor and dying on each continent."

The airplane taxied to the runway, and the two women began to pray, their voices a low murmur. Though Jim considered himself a ho-hum Catholic who went to church mostly out of habit, inexplicably he found himself joining in. By the time they murmured the final prayer, the plane had reached cruising altitude.

Mother Teresa turned toward him. For the first time in his life, Jim understood what people meant when they spoke of a person possessing an aura. As she gazed at him, a sense of peace filled him; he could no more see it than he could see the wind, but he felt it, just as surely as he felt a warm summer breeze. "Young man," she inquired, "do you say the Rosary often?"

Later, as he described his encounter, Jim laughed sheepishly. "You don't lie to Mother Teresa!" So he admitted, "No, not really."

She took his hand, while her eyes probed his. Then she smiled. "Well, you will now." And she dropped her rosary into his palm.

An hour later, Jim entered the Kansas City airport, where he was met by his wife Ruth. "What in the world—?" began Ruth, as she noticed the rosary in his hand. They kissed and Jim described his encounter. Driving home, he said, "I feel as if I met a true sister of God." Reverently, he placed Mother Teresa's rosary on his bedroom dresser.

If that were the end of the story, it might be story enough, but nine months later, Jim and Ruth visited Connie, a longtime friend of theirs. Connie confided that she'd been told she had ovarian cancer. "The doctors say it's a tough case, but I'm going to fight it. I won't give up!"

Jim clasped her hand. Then, after reaching into his pocket, he gently twined Mother Teresa's rosary around her fingers. He told her the story and said, "Keep it with you, Connie. It may help." Although Connie wasn't Catholic, her hand closed willingly around the small plastic beads. "Thank you," she whispered. "I hope I can return it."

More than a year passed before Jim saw Connie again. This time, face glowing, she hurried toward him and handed him the rosary. "I carried it with me all year," she said, and hesitated, as if searching for words. "I've had surgery and been on chemotherapy, too. Last month, the doctors did 'second look' surgery and the tumor's gone. Completely!" Her eyes met Jim's. "I knew it was time to give the rosary back."

A few months later, Jim got a call from Bill, an attorney he knew. Bill had heard about the rosary from a mutual friend and he asked if he could borrow it before an upcoming trial. "I know my client is innocent," explained Bill, "but it's going to be hard trying to convince the jury. I think the rosary will help." Did Bill's faith, as he fingered the small plastic beads, bring out his best when he walked into the courtroom? Whatever the reason, he argued so convincingly that his client was acquitted. "Thanks," he said simply when he returned the rosary.

In the fall of 1987, Ruth's sister Liz fell into a deep depression after her divorce. She asked Jim if she could borrow the rosary and when he sent it, she hung it over her bedpost in a small velvet bag.

"At night, I held on to it, just physically held on. I was so lonely and afraid," she admitted. "Yet, when I gripped that rosary, I felt as if I held a loving hand." Gradually, Liz pulled her life together and she mailed the rosary back. "Someone else may need it," she said.

Then one night in 1988 a stranger telephoned Ruth. She'd heard about the rosary from a neighbor and asked if she could borrow it to take to the hospital where her mother lay in a coma. The family hoped the rosary might help their mother die peacefully.

A few days later, the woman returned the beads. "The nurses told me a coma patient can still hear," she said, "so I explained to my mother that I had Mother Teresa's rosary and that when I gave it to her, she could let go; it would be all right. Then I put the rosary in her hand. Right away, we saw her face relax! The lines smoothed out until she looked so peaceful. So young." The woman's voice caught, and a tear slid down her cheek. "A few minutes later . . . she was gone." Fervently, she gripped Ruth's hands. "Thank you."

Requests continued to come, often unexpectedly. Whenever Jim gave the rosary to someone, he always said, "When you're through needing it, send it back for someone else." The rosary always came back.

Jim's own life changed after his unexpected meeting on the airplane. No longer is he a ho-hum Christian. "Mother Teresa helped me understand love in a new way," he says. After she told Jim she saw Christ disguised in every diseased, dying person, Jim began to look in a new way at the people he met.

When he realized Mother Teresa carries everything she owns in a small bag, Jim made an effort to simplify his own life. "I try to remember what really counts — not money or titles or possessions, but the way we love others," he remarks.

And what about Mother Teresa's rosary? Is there special power in those humble beads? Or is the power of the Holy Spirit renewed in each person who borrows the rosary? Do we all have the power if we open ourselves to it? What do you think?

25
My Father's Last Gift

The hospital room percolates softly with the sound of the respirator. It sounds like a coffeepot instead of a machine to keep my father alive. Carefully, I step around the other life-support machines, push aside an IV bag, tilt slightly on my toes, and touch my father's face. California dawn creeps gently through the window blinds.

"How is he?" I ask.

"Blood pressure has dropped," says Polly, the night nurse. We have come to know them all in the three weeks my father has lain critically ill: Judy, Colleen, Tom, Polly, J.P.

Polly glances at her thick charts, as if hoping to find something she missed. "Otherwise, no real change, I'm afraid."

I squeeze my father's hand. It rests slackly in mine, the strong square hand that could open any jar, toss any ball, rumple a grandchild's hair. "Daddy, it's me," I plead. "Can you open your eyes? Please? For me?"

But his face, so yellow, stays empty and closed. Only the furrows of pain seem to deepen. Behind the percolating respirator, I hear soft gurgles and the blipping sound of the heart monitor. Tubes run into my father's nose, feed into his arms, drip into the cushions of his shoulders.

It should have been simple surgery. A heart bypass is not unusual these days. We had all telephoned Daddy the night before, all his children and grandchildren. My son Andy said, "You're gonna be out of surgery at 2:30, Granddaddy? That's great. I'll call you at three."

His grandfather's hearty chuckle had spun across the telephone wires. "What do you think this is, a little Novocain job?" He was still laughing, repeating the story to the anesthesiologist, as they wheeled him into the operating room.

Maybe he wouldn't be talking by three, his laughter seemed to say, but he sure expected to feel good soon.

He sure didn't plan on a heart attack during surgery.

Polly reaches around me to place ice bags beneath my father's arm. Before, he would flinch at the sudden cold. Now, he doesn't stir. The hospital makes morning noises. A stainless-steel breakfast cart clatters. Voices rise as nursing shifts change. I hear the familiar rubber wheels of the portable X-ray machine, coming to my father.

I kiss his forehead. "I'll be right back, Daddy." He doesn't stir.

In the central core of the ICU unit, nurses swap charts. Monitors hooked to the critical-care rooms spin green designs across their screens.

Dr. Ip — the young Chinese surgeon who is coordinating all the doctors now attending my father, specialists in kidneys and liver and blood and infection and brain and heart — strides down the corridor, his white coat swishing.

"I am just looking in on your father," he says in his precise, gentle way. "There is fear we have more infection from the surgical incision."

"Oh, no! What will you do?"

"Ordinarily, we take the patient back to OR and reopen the wound, clean it out . . . but your father is so sick . . . his liver is so damaged . . ."

I hear hesitation in his voice. A pause. The X-ray machine whirs down the hall on its rubber wheels. Something heavy and suffocating, like wet cotton balls, clogs my throat. I go to the phones and call my mother.

When she reaches my father's bedside, she pats his face, clasps his hand. "Cy, it's Erna. And today is my birthday. You're going to get better today, remember? You always gave me such nice birthday presents. This year's will be the very best because you're going to get better." She shakes his slack hand. "Do you hear me, Cy?" I see Judy, the day nurse, turn away.

The door opens. My sister-in-law comes in. Eileen is a nurse, too, and Judy whispers to her, one nurse to another.

"Mom," says Eileen.

My mother is gently touching the bandage that covers the infected surgical wound. "He's so yellow," she sighs. She raises herself on tiptoes — she stands a full head shorter than my tall, big-boned father — and pleads: "Cy, open your eyes now, Cy. Come on, please. For my birthday. Come on . . ."

"Mom," says Eileen. She looks at me. I know she loves my father. In ten years of living just a few miles apart, she's come to know her father-in-law well.

"Mom," she says gently, "he's not going to make it."

I see the awareness in my mother's eyes.

"More surgery will only give him pain."

The cotton balls clog my throat so I can barely speak. Slowly, my mother nods. "Better call your brothers." The respirator percolates softly.

They have shut the door to my father's room. The priest has come and gone. Judy closes the slatted blinds that cover the windows to the corridor. She offers to bring coffee. No one responds.

"We are stopping the dopamine that has maintained your father's blood pressure. Nature will take over," Dr. Ip tells us. Quietly, Judy unplugs two tubes. "Because his liver is so damaged and cannot properly excrete the dopamine in his system, it could be twelve hours. Or much sooner. But we can give your father morphine now, so he will not feel pain."

My brothers and I and my mother and Eileen gather around my father's bed.

My mother holds Daddy's right hand.

My brother Jack stands with one hand on our father's arm. His eyes are hidden behind dark glasses. His shoulders shake as he tries to keep his emotions under control.

My younger brother, Rob, stands beside me. He seems unaware he is weeping.

I hold Daddy's other hand. Tightly.

Another nod from Dr. Ip and Judy inserts a syringe. The gurgling stops. She takes away the IV feeding bag. Only the percolating respirator goes on. And the soft blip of the heart monitor.

Daddy! my heart cries. *Daddy, don't leave us!* Then, as the morphine takes effect, I see the pain lines smooth. His mouth closes, his yellowed face takes on a new, more peaceful contour.

My mother leans forward. Her voice has a different timbre, the vulnerable sound of a young girl. "Cy, do you feel better now? It doesn't hurt so much, does it?" Her hand pats his cheek. "I fixed the brakes on the car, you know, just like you wanted."

Rob sobs.

The afternoon spins slowly out. Like summertime, I think, when I was a child and time seemed forever. Our voices drift like currents of air. "I'm so glad the family got together last year . . ."

"The grandkids had such a great time with their grandfather . . ."

"So many get-well cards. He'd be pleased . . ."

An orderly comes in to take blood.

Rob shakes his head. "No need now."

The air seems heavy. It presses on my lungs like the humid pressure before a Midwest thunderstorm. Still holding Daddy's hand, I sit down and lean my head on my arms.

The clock moves slowly past five.

Dr. Ip has returned. He glances at the heart monitor. "Blood pressure reads 32. When it drops below 30, it won't be long."

The cotton balls are back in my throat. I lean forward and kiss Daddy's forehead. "You know . . ." — my laugh is shaky; I can feel the tears beneath — "I keep thinking about Daddy's photos."

"I'll bet he's filled fifty albums."

"Always a surprise to open one of Dad's albums. You never know what you'll find."

"He said it kept things interesting." We laugh.

"Dad has a crazy sense of humor. He told the boys that the rocks in the San Diego hills are growing."

"And they'd grow faster if we played them rock music."

Dr. Ip's laughter joins ours. "I would like to have known your father . . ."

The room falls silent.

"I remember," muses Rob, "how he always said, 'It doesn't matter where you start . . .' " The rest of us chorus, " 'It's where you finish that counts.' "

"All those years he went to night school."

"Taught me a lot about hanging in there. And believing in myself."

The clock creeps past seven.

Rob strides down the hall to call his wife. Halfway to the phone, there's a shout. "Hurry, blood pressure's dropped below 30!"

He races back and then, inexplicably, blood pressure stabilizes.

Another hour passes.

We wait.

Dr. Ip waits, too. He must be off-duty by now, I think. How nice of him to stay with us. My brothers watch the heart monitor. I watch my father's face. And my mother's.

I remember Daddy's phone call, a few months earlier. It was evening then, too. "Just sitting in my study," he said, in the rich deep tones that could sing or give an order or tell a joke, all equally well, "and I found myself thinking how proud of you I am. How much I love you. So I decided to call and tell you. What d'ya think about that?"

My brother Jack gasps. My mother leans forward. Her lips brush my father's cheek as she whispers, "Good-bye, Cy. God bless you."

The monitor's green line has gone straight; the respirator is silent.

I'm surprised at how gentle death is. I know grief waits beyond the threshold, but all I feel now is peace. I squeeze my father's hand a final time. "I love you, too, Daddy." Somehow, in that hushed room, I think he knows.

26

The Magic Word for 'God Within'

One way to find God's answer in our lives is to look with enthusiasm, to open ourselves up to what excites us. Joseph Campbell, the mythologist, put it this way: "Follow your bliss."

Are you following yours?

Or are you pursuing the career — the way of life — your parents said you "should" follow? Are you wedded to a job because it's secure? Do you sometimes feel like Dorothy in Kansas, living a black-and-white life instead of the joyful color of Oz?

A wise adviser once told me, "Barbara, enthusiasm will take you farther than any amount of experience or training."

How right he was! Enthusiastic people can turn a boring drive into an adventure, extra work into opportunity, and a city of strangers into a city of friends.

"Nothing great was ever achieved without enthusiasm," wrote Ralph Waldo Emerson. Enthusiasm is the sticky paste that helps you hang in there when the going gets tough. It's the inner voice that mutters, "I can do it! I can do it!" when others around you shout, "No, you can't!"

Dr. Barbara McClintock, a geneticist who won the 1983 Nobel Prize for Medicine, was ignored by her peers for nearly forty years. Yet she never let up on her experiments. "Work has been such a deep pleasure that I never thought of stopping," she explained, "and I just hated sleeping. I can't imagine having a better life."

Declares Dr. Paul Tournier, a Swiss psychiatrist, "Enthusiasm is the state of mind of a person engaged in an adventure."

We cannot *acquire* enthusiasm, we can only *rediscover* it. We are all born with wide-eyed, enthusiastic wonder. I see it in my grandson Nathan as he plays with his mother's car keys. Or in Danny, a chunky toddler exploring the outdoors. With what wonder his curious eyes will spy a scurrying beetle!

It's this childlike wonder that gives enthusiastic people such a youthful air, whatever their age. Norman Cousins in *Anatomy of an Illness* describes the enthusiasm of the cellist Pablo Casals in his later years. Casals, at ninety, would start his day by playing Bach, and as the music flowed through his fingers, writes Cousins, his aged shoulders would straighten and joy would reappear in his eyes. Music, for Casals, was an elixir that made life a never-ending adventure.

How do you rediscover the enthusiasm of your childhood? If life seems like a black-and-white movie, how do you recolor it?

I think the answer lies in the word itself. *Enthusiasm* comes from the Greek *en theo* and means "God within." And what is "God within" but an abiding sense of love — a nurturing love of self and, from that, love of others?

People who care enough about themselves to pursue what they love exude enthusiasm.

It has nothing to do with money earned or title or power. Dr. Patricia McIlrath, former director of the Missouri Repertory Theatre in Kansas City, was asked, "Where do you get your enthusiasm?" She replied, "My father was a lawyer. Long ago, he told me, 'I never made a dime until I stopped working for money.' "

Each of us needs to discover what it is that we *love* to do. If it can't be a full-time career, it can be a part-time avocation: the prime minister who paints on Sunday, the nun who runs marathons, the mother who joins an amateur theater, the executive who handcrafts furniture.

Elizabeth Layton of Topeka, Kansas, was sixty-seven before she began painting. This activity ended fits of depression that had plagued her for thirty years, and the quality of her work is such that one critic said, "I am tempted to call Layton a genius." Elizabeth rediscovered her enthusiasm.

Mary Jo Richards lost her husband in a way that's almost as painful as death. After sixteen years of marriage, he left her for another woman. Mary Jo was devastated, and on a practical level, she wondered how to support their four children, all enrolled in parochial schools. Then she discovered that she loved to sell — and her enthusiasm for selling computers eventually made her one of IBM's top ten salespeople.

I think "self-acceptance" is a good synonym for the shining discovery of "God within." That shine puts a sparkle in our eye, a lilt in our step, and smooths out any "wrinkles" in our souls.

"God within" also refers to those talents we receive at birth, whether they be the talents of a Nobel Prize winner or of a parent who has enthusiastically reared six children.

Robert Frost in *Two Tramps in Mud Time* wrote:

My object in living is to unite
My avocation and my vocation
As my two eyes make one in sight.

To unite your avocation and vocation, always look forward, not back. Don't waste precious tears on "might have beens." Turn the tears into sweat as you go after "what can be."

Enthusiasm will help you to hang in through the tough times. As Edwin Way Teale says in *Circle of Seasons,* the true measure of a person's enthusiasm must be taken *between* interesting events. "It is between bites," says Teale, "that the lukewarm angler loses heart."

Learn to appreciate life's miniature rainbows. True enthusiasts find pleasure in the fragrance of a backyard garden or the orange-crayoned picture of a six-year-old. Live in the present moment. Take time to *be*, so your sense can bring home all that you are experiencing at that moment. Once we appreciate life's smaller rainbows, we rediscover the larger ones.

Most of all, remember that everyone's life holds the unexpected. The unexpected joy, and the unexpected sorrow. When we greet the unexpected with enthusiasm — that is, with faith in "God within" — we will find answers that go beyond any of our own imaginings.